What industry leaders are saying about

TELL YOUR CLIENTS WHERE TO GO!

"Wow! Todd Sebastian has prescribed beautifully the dream agency partner. This truly is a passionate and practical perspective on what it means to be a real agency partner. Now all we need is the companion guide for the dream client."

Joey Bergstein
SVP Global Marketing, I
Diageo

"Can simple, practical perspective really make you a better agency partner? Yes, and Todd Sebastian's *Tell Your Clients Where to Go!* shows you how. Just like today's consumers who pay a premium for 'experiences' and become loyal to such, Todd passionately brings to life 20 years of on-the-job learning and shows how easy it is for you to move beyond transactional relationships to reach a true strategic partnership with your clients. And this is an 'experience' your clients will value, leading to long-term success for your agency, your clients and you personally."

Scott Rogers
Senior Vice President, Marketing & Sales
Norwegian Cruise Line

"Todd Sebastian nails it in *Tell Your Clients Where to Go!* Effective agency partners have to provide more than a checklist of services; they must invest themselves ardently in the end benefit of growing the business. He understands that you can't wait around for clients to call, and offers a blueprint for account team success that focuses on attention to detail, the proactive offering of ideas, and deep personal involvement in the business."

Todd Rywolt
VP of Marketing, New Business Development
Hasbro

"Having worked with agencies over the last 18 years, Todd Sebastian has done a great job summarizing what it takes to make a great agency partner. At the end of the day a great partner artfully balances when to take the lead and when to follow the client. Great relationships deliver work the client needs to deliver the business. The practical suggestions offered by Todd really enable that."

Kirk L. Perry
VP/General Manager, North America Baby Care
Procter & Gamble

"Whether you're a novice or seasoned veteran in this business, Todd Sebastian's *Tell Your Clients Where to Go!* offers insightful and practical lessons, enabling us all to become better devotees of 'passionate partnership'!"

Greg A. Zimmer
Chief Brand Designer
3M

"Todd's book *Tell Your Clients Where to Go!* is brimming with helpful, practical advice for any client-facing person in almost any field. He provides very specific, actionable tips — things account people can begin to do differently or better right away, as in today. Todd's passion for 'agency life' and his clients' businesses is obvious. While this is a perfect read for anyone starting out in a client-facing role, it's a great refresher course for experienced practitioners, as well. Client 'service' is one thing, but Todd reminds us that it is leadership that is truly valued and valuable."

Mary Zalla
Managing Director, Cincinnati and Chicago
Landor Associates

"Todd Sebastian serves up a highly practical guide to surprising your clients with proactive partnership. He cuts through the glut of 'theory-based' books by offering actionable advice rooted in real-world experience."

Todd Henry
President
Accidental Creative

"Todd Sebastian's *Tell Your Clients Where to Go!* reminds us of the fundamentals in agency account service. As the nature of business changes and technology continues to evolve, more than ever we need a practical perspective on being a passionate and proactive partner to our clients. Todd's book is an essential call-to-action for success in account service."

Jerry Kathman
President & CEO
LPK

"Todd Sebastian is one of the most accomplished and successful agency leaders in the business. His *Tell Your Clients Where to Go!* is an inside view into how he has transformed relationships, grown client businesses and raised the bar for account people. This book is required reading for my teammates and should be a must-read for any account person."

Amanda Skerski
Director, Client Partnerships
WONGDOODY

"With experience on both sides of the fence, Todd Sebastian is a living, breathing example of excellence in building and sustaining positive, long-lasting agency-client partnerships. *Tell Your Clients Where to Go!* is highly recommended reading for anyone seeking *the* authoritative source for the qualities and skills you need to be a stellar agency partner."

Ric Sweeney
MS-Marketing Program Director, University of Cincinnati
Board of Trustees, American Marketing Association Foundation

"Having worked for Todd, I was able to see the principles in *Tell Your Clients Where to Go!* in action. Through his passion and experience, Todd gave me the tools I needed to become a true strategic partner for my clients. His insights and guidance can take any account person's skills to the next level."

Rob Jones
Account Leader
Interbrand

"Todd Sebastian shaped years of hands-on experience into a fantastic, indispensable guide on what it takes to be a successful agency partner. The advice is practical, the author is passionate, and the result is a highly readable, and more importantly actionable, guide to improving the leadership you provide your clients. I've made this book mandatory reading for everyone on our account team."

Doug Worple
CEO
BAREFOOT (A BBDO Company)

"*Tell Your Clients Where to Go!* causes anyone who reads it to take a long look in the mirror and re-evaluate the value that they add to their clients, and therefore to their own company, on an everyday basis. Todd Sebastian's book should be viewed as the definitive training manual for client service professionals in any agency discipline. In sharing his experiences and philosophies, we all benefit from a career's worth of learning and results. This book is mandatory reading for anyone who joins our company."

Mark T. Macchiarulo
President
Amplitude Marketing Group

"After reading Todd Sebastian's *Tell Your Clients Where to Go!* I have approached each day by asking myself how I can be a better agency partner. Account management is a demanding job with many responsibilities and roles, and this book helped me focus on refining the mindset and skills that are essential for becoming a strong leader. Todd's personal examples, some of which I experienced first-hand as a member of his account team, truly illustrate how showing passion in your clients' businesses leads to invaluable partnerships."

Kelly Tholke
Account Executive
TBWA\Chiat\Day

"A lot of companies claim they use superior service to distinguish themselves from competitors, but few can back that up with specifics. *Tell Your Clients Where to Go!* is the play book that provides those service specifics. Todd Sebastian relates common sense guidelines on how to achieve your own success through building your client's business, and backs them with relevant, timely examples."

Lisa Biank Fasig
Reporter
Cincinnati Business Courier

"I found Todd Sebastian's *Tell Your Clients Where to Go!* to be a very practical roadmap for developing lasting client relationships. Having worked with Todd, I can assure you that he has lived every bit of advice he is sharing. Todd was truly a partner. He always came to the table with the mindset of doing 'the best for the brand,' was passionate about what he believed in, and a fantastic person with whom to work!"

Ena Singh
Senior Manager, Oncology Marketing
GlaxoSmithKline

TELL YOUR CLIENTS WHERE TO GO!

TELL YOUR CLIENTS WHERE TO GO!

A Practical Guide to Providing Passionate Client Leadership

TODD SEBASTIAN

ISBN 0-7414-4903-X

Cover design by Tim Fening, Principal/Chief Creative Officer of CAUSE Agency

Edited by LinDee Rochelle

Published by:

1094 New DeHaven Street, Suite 100
West Conshohocken, PA 19428-2713
Info@buybooksontheweb.com
www.buybooksontheweb.com
Toll-free (877) BUY BOOK
Local Phone (610) 941-9999
Fax (610) 941-9959

Printed in the United States of America

Printed on Recycled Paper

Published August 2008

TO KATHY.

I appreciate your support

as I pursue my passion.

I love you.

Contents

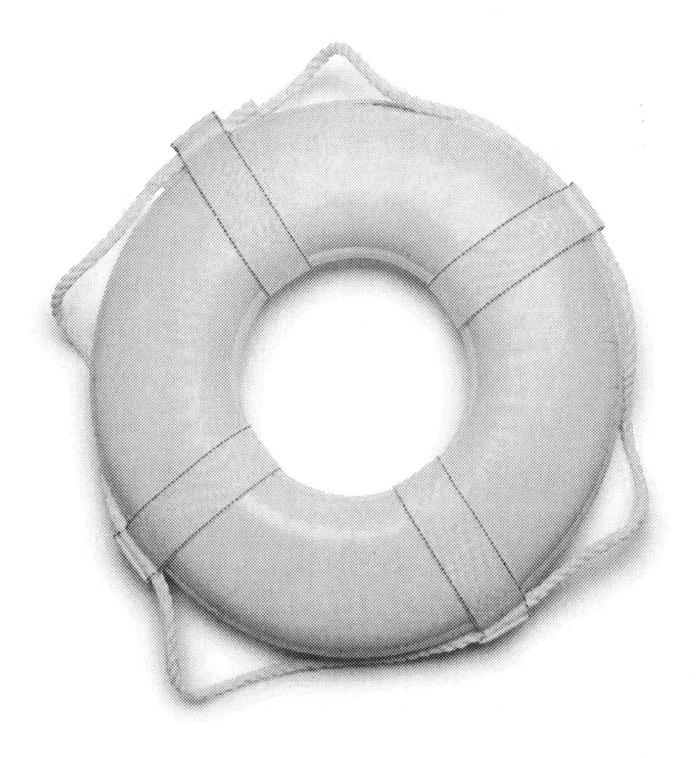

Sink or swim. Sadly, this idiomatic expression serves as the philosophical background for the way in which many of us learn how to become successful professionals in the marketing and communications field. In our industry there's a pervasive belief that you can't really *teach* someone how to establish and nurture productive client relationships. You just have to step in there and learn on the job. At best, some may be lucky and have kindhearted bosses whose junior staffers "shadow" them for a time. Eventually, however, it most often comes down to sink or swim.

In my career's early days I was fortunate to be counseled by an amazing mentor. He coached me and taught me about business, people, and how to maintain effective, professional relationships with everyone from the reception desk to the CEO's office. One day at lunch the phrase "sink or swim" came up in our conversation. I'll always remember his take on that philosophy. With a twinkle in his eye, he wisely noted, "Gary, the problem with sink or swim is that a very high percentage of potentially powerful swimmers will drown because they were never given swimming lessons. We owe it to our industry to give swimming lessons."

When I was in graduate school, some of us would sarcastically taunt our more jaded professors with the cliché, "Those who can, DO. Those who can't, TEACH!" At times many of these academicians seemed aloof, living in a theoretical world that was devoid of real-life experiences. Such is not the case with Todd Sebastian.

In *Tell Your Clients Where to Go!* he pulls from his past — and current — experiences as one of our industry's finest "doers." But more than that he is an exceptionally-talented "teacher." His heartfelt passion for "beginning swimmers" is clearly apparent in this comprehensive yet simple, step-by-step guide to earning a Gold Medal in the Client Relations Olympics.

But this wealth of information shouldn't be limited to entry-level managers. As a 25-year+ veteran, I found this book to be an invaluable refresher course. I think you will, too. It is a reminder of the things that really matter in fostering productive partnerships with clients and co-workers, alike.

We live in an era when many of the "great ones" have passed. The legends whose names and initials adorn the signage of our offices have left us: e.g., Walter Landor, Saul Bass, Bill Bernbach, and David Ogilvy. And with no intention of slighting current industry leaders, I believe our field is moving away from human icons and replacing them with ideas, as a type of collective classroom. And I would propose that books like this one will become the new mentors of best practices. As such, I should stop writing and let you start reading. With each sentence I'm keeping you away from this storehouse of information. But I must indulge you with a personal reference.

During my tenure as chief creative officer of Interbrand's Cincinnati office, I stood side-by-side with Todd in many a meeting. From a first-hand vantage point I watched him develop enduring relationships with his clients, staff and co-workers. I witnessed his words in action as troubled accounts became enthusiastic evangelists and advocates of his leadership. Naturally, I was flattered (and humbled) when he invited me to write this foreword. But I deemed it an honor, if not a responsibility, to wholeheartedly endorse the importance of this book and the man who wrote it.

Many a hopeful "swimmer" will benefit from this offering, whether beginners or experienced. Seasoned executives will not only benefit as well, but additionally find *Tell Your Clients Where to Go!* to be a timely primer for coaching their teams. So with Todd as your instructor, and his insights as your life vest, jump in the pool. The water's warm, and you're not going to drown.

Gary Whitlock
Director of Brand Strategy and Design
ChaseDesign, San Francisco

ser·vice [sər·vəs] *noun*

the system or operation by which people are provided with something they need or request

(source: Merriam-Webster's dictionary)

---

ac·count ser·vic·es [ə-kaünt sər·vəs·es] *noun*

an agency's staff of "order takers," who provide client service but lack leadership

(source: Many frustrated clients)

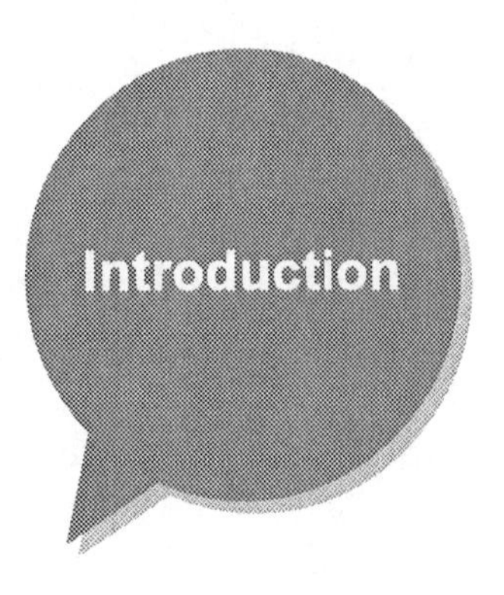

The word "service" reeks of reactive behavior. Someone asks for something and someone else responds by filling the request. When client service providers remain in this reactionary mode — *as too many do* — they are seen as nothing more than "order takers" by their clients. They traffic work back and forth listlessly between agencies and clients. They provide clients what is requested — *but nothing more.* They are seen as old-fashioned sales people who simply take and fill orders. They are not perceived as adding value. They form transactional relationships, not strategic partnerships.

It doesn't help matters when the word "service" is embedded in the name of the team: account or client services, which is usually led by a director of client services. This simply reinforces and perpetuates clients' sub-optimal expectations of client service providers and the agencies they represent.

To begin the process of exceeding clients' expectations, two things need to happen. First, immediately remove "service" from the name of your team and your vernacular. You may not have any control over the official designation used within your agency, but you can control how you describe your role to your clients. Rather than account services or client services, try account team or client leadership team. If you do have control over the official title, make the change official, at the earliest opportunity. This will create a more positive external perception and it will yield internal benefits, as well. The word "team" suggests that the members can and should be working together and learning from one another. Even though everyone on the team has assigned clients for whom they are personally responsible and accountable, it shouldn't be an "everyone is on their own" situation. When a client account is particularly busy or facing trouble, people not assigned to the account should be offering to help — even if just behind-the-scenes. The client service provider who received help from the other team members will be more than happy to return the favor down the road.

More importantly, everyone in a client service role needs to dramatically shift their mindsets. This may not be easy, but it is necessary. Client service providers need to move beyond simply "providing service." They need to understand the leadership role they play in building client partnerships for their agencies — and they need to attack this role in a passionate, proactive and consultative manner.

Tell Your Clients Where to Go! *focuses first on this mandatory mindset shift* — *and the positive impact it will have on client partnerships*. Other books for client service providers focus only on fundamentals. This book will review fundamentals, too, by discussing the qualities and skills you need to develop, and proven practical tips you can employ, in order to put these qualities and skills into practice successfully. But, if you don't start with the right mindset, the rest won't matter. A model mindset provides the foundation upon which to build the proper fundamentals.

Accordingly, the framework of this book is a simple 3-step approach to becoming a high-impact partner to your clients:

- Step 1: Start with a model mindset.
- Step 2: Develop quintessential qualities and skills.
- Step 3: Apply proven practical tips.

The third step comprises the majority of this book. It is full of practical tips you can start employing today. These tips are brought to life with a plethora of successful examples in which I have participated or witnessed firsthand.

Who am I?

Brand management at Procter & Gamble motivated the first third of my nearly 20-year career in the marketing and communications industry. Then, I switched to the agency side — including advertising, branding and design, influencer marketing, and shopper/consumer insights. Throughout, it is my honor to have led large agencies and multi-functional agency teams — including account managers, strategic planners, analysts and creatives. On the agency side of the business my responsibilities have included titles of vice president, chief account officer, and executive director of North America.

In every agency I worked P&G was our biggest client — so it has been, and continues to be, the client with which I spend the majority of my time. I love it. P&G is an incredibly demanding and challenging client, as it should be. To be successful with this type of dynamic client, you cannot simply provide adequate client service and mechanically deliver what is asked of you. You need to demonstrate constant and consistent passion for their amazing brands and the ability to add true value to the work. If you are successful in doing so, the client feedback and the results can be exhilarating and extremely fulfilling.

Why am I writing this book?

A very strong passion drives me to work with challenging clients and develop strong partnerships. I also feel strongly about continually learning and growing — and encouraging others to stretch their reach, too. I have been successful in my career by being passionate and proactive — and I want to show you how you can, too. I love coaching and training. It is, by far, the most fulfilling part of my job.

I am not writing this book to become rich! In fact, all of my income from *Tell Your Clients Where to Go!* is donated to charity. I simply enjoy helping others, and believe I have some client leadership experience and perspective with which to mentor.

Who is it for?

If you want to captivate your clients and catapult your career, this book is for you. It is relevant to any industry — but indispensable for people who work in advertising agencies, marketing consultancies and any other professional service firms.

While it is primarily intended for account people, this book is perfectly appropriate for *anyone who is the least bit client facing in their role.* If you engage with clients to any degree you have an impact on the perceptions they form of your agency — and, thus, on the quality of the partnerships your agency builds with them.

Furthermore, while this book is largely intended to serve as a training tool for those in the early stages of their career, it can also be a great refresher — with a unique perspective — for even the most senior leaders. Many senior-level managers generously reviewed the manuscript for this book. Almost all of them shared with me the fact that they were reminded of client leadership fundamentals which they realized they had forgotten — or don't practice as much as they should.

Tell Your Clients Where to Go! also provides valuable perspective for people on the client side of the relationship. It will help clients interact with their agencies and provide a valuable tool with which to discuss and agree on partnership-related expectations. In addition, this book will guide clients to more passionately and proactively lead their own clients — including their managers, shareholders, trade customers and consumers.

Since this book is applicable to a large number of professional roles that involve the management of clients, I will apply the term "client leader" from this point forward. This term casts a net on anyone who wants to more effectively lead their clients and build stronger partnerships with them.

What can you expect to discover here?

I want to share a *practical perspective* on how to be a *passionate* and *proactive partner* to your clients. I have carefully chosen each of these words. Therefore, let me explain my choices briefly, and thus crystallize what I hope you will obtain from this book:

- *Practical. Tell Your Clients …* discusses the mindset, qualities and skills you need to develop to become a strong client leader; *and* it provides specific and practical tips that you can apply through practice every day. I bring these tips to life with real examples of success stories that led to improved client partnerships.

  In addition to offering advice that is practical, I tried to make the book itself practical. My hope is that you will reference it routinely. To make that process as easy as possible, I organized the book into a simple 3-step process. Its practical tips are formatted in bullet-point fashion to make each nugget of information easy to find, digest and remember.

- *Perspective.* This is not intended to be the definitive "how-to," but rather a unique perspective — based on personal experience as a successful leader on both the agency and client sides of the industry. I encourage you to consider this perspective, along with guidance from other people who have been successful. I am certainly not claiming to be the highest authority on this topic. But, I have been in this business a long time. I have learned extensively from great agency leaders and fantastic client partners; and I have developed my own unique points of view. I simply want to pass my experience and advice on to you to add to your overall base of perspective.

- *Passionate.* If you are not passionate about building client partnerships, you should seriously consider a new career. If you are, show it! This book provides perspective and practical tips on how to show your passion effectively.

- *Proactive.* Too many client leaders simply *react* to client needs. Therefore, they are seen as nothing more than "order takers" by their clients. True agency partners are proactive, not reactive. They anticipate needs and exceed expectations. This book will discuss the importance of, and approach to, providing the leadership your clients crave.

- *Partner.* Your actions as a client leader should not be focused only on providing good "client service." You need to become an indispensable business partner to your clients. *That's what clients want.* Survey after survey among clients confirms this point. True partnership-oriented behavior among agency people is ranked consistently as one of the strongest desires of clients and, unfortunately, one of the biggest perceived inadequacies. And keep in mind that it "takes two to tango." So, if you want your clients to act like partners and treat you like a partner, you need to behave like one. As you strive to build strong client partnerships, you should never be satisfied with what you deem success. This leads to complacency. Strive to continually build and strengthen your client partnerships. The ultimate goal of this book is to show you how you can become the best partner possible to your clients.

Be passionate and proactive. These qualities will help you to become a strong partner to your clients and they will set you apart from the horde of "order takers" out there. But, the first step in becoming an outstanding partner is adopting a model mindset. This is the focus of the following first section.

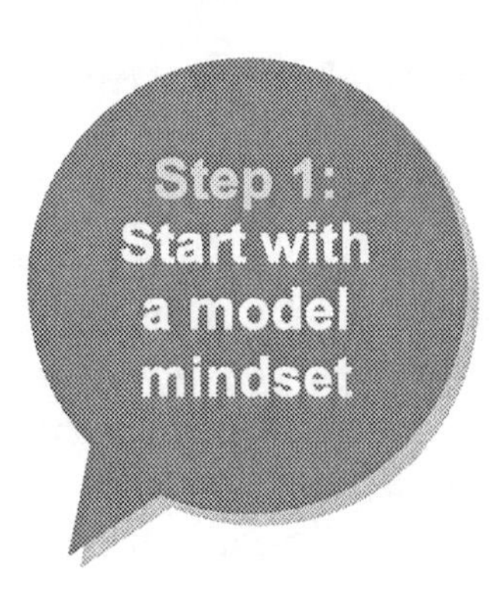

Here's a trivia question for you:

How often is San Francisco's Golden Gate Bridge painted?

a. Every year.
b. Every 5 years.
c. Every 10 years.
d. Every 25 years.

The answer:

e. None of the above.

Painting the Golden Gate Bridge is an *on-going* task. It is the "face" of San Francisco. As a result, the city wants the bridge to always look its best in order to create a strong impression and draw new visitors. To do so, a discreet work crew is positioned perpetually on the bridge for routine painting to *continually improve* its appearance.

Agencies have goals similar to this example. In particular, they share the desire to continually improve their perceptions with their current clients and to grow their business by attracting new clients.

Client leaders play a significant leadership role in achieving both of these important goals. They are the faces of their agencies — just as the Golden Gate Bridge is the face of San Francisco.

All client leaders — and anyone else in a client-facing role — should keep this visual metaphor top-of-mind. *It represents the mindset with which you should approach everything you do*. You need to think before you act. This section provides perspective on how you should mentally approach your critically-important role.

Concentrate on continual improvement

You cannot become complacent. You need to constantly improve your skill set and performance level in order to lead your accounts, to continually improve your client partnerships, and to represent your agency as successfully as possible.

The first step in continual improvement is to thoroughly review your job description. You need to know what is expected of you, agree with it, and focus your energies on delivering against it. If you don't have a job description — and there is an alarming number of agency people who don't — make it a priority to acquire one. Obtain your manager's approval and write it yourself if necessary. Make sure it captures detailed definitions of your position's purpose, essential functions, and required experience, knowledge, skills and abilities.

Once you have done this, secure a copy of the job description for the position *above* you. This will impart invaluable insight into what it will take to secure a promotion. Once you understand this, start doing it! The best way to attain the next level is to perform at that level. Doing so makes your promotion a "no-brainer" for your manager — and you will undoubtedly provide increased value to your clients in the process.

Another key step in continual improvement is adhering to your work & development plan. Again, if you don't have one, obtain one. Immediately. It is critically important to have a plan that challenges and pushes you to improve your performance, and to deliver improved results for your clients.

As you create your work & development plan, you need to be introspective and self-critical. Be honest with yourself with regard to the areas in which you need to improve — then seek help to implement change. Take control of your plan, enlist your manager as a partner and tell him or her where you need help. It is critical to make sure your objectives are clear and to have an agree-to plan on how to deliver against them.

To avoid any misunderstanding regarding your performance objectives and level of success, make sure your work & development plan captures the following in some fashion:

- *Goals:* Prioritize 3-5 goals you want to accomplish in the forthcoming year. This list should include personals goals, as well as goals that pertain to your clients' businesses. If your clients are not succeeding, neither are you.

- *Strengths:* Identify 3-5 existing strengths upon which you want to continue to focus and build.

- *Development areas:* List 3-5 specific areas in which you need to demonstrate significant growth. To make this development plan as actionable as possible, define the following with extreme specificity:

    - *Your action plans:* Outline the specific actions you commit to take to improve in these areas. Be clear on what success looks like.

- *Your manager's action plans:* In order for you to succeed, your manager must take an active role. Insist on this. Identify the tools, training and help you need from your manager in order for you to deliver on your commitments.

- *Timing:* Set a timeline for completion of actions and measurement of your performance against your going-in objectives.

Your work & development plan should include formal training. Take advantage of every internal and external opportunity afforded to you. You can never become too good for your role — particularly in areas such as leadership, communication, presentation skills, negotiating, strategic thinking and relationship building.

Beyond formal training, you should seek out informal day-to-day training, advice and feedback from your management, your clients and your peers. Do so constantly and relentlessly. Asking for help is a sign of strength, not weakness.

If you are passionate about what you do and you take your role seriously, concentrating on continual self-improvement will come much more naturally and easily. You will want to improve continually the way in which you represent your agency and deliver value for your clients.

Appreciate the power of perception

As the primary face of agencies, client leaders control the impressions their clients form. Therefore, everything you do — however big or small — reflects upon your agency and impacts your clients' perceptions of it. Everything from a very sound and strategic business-building proposal to a short e-mail strewn with typos can and will have an impact — good or bad.

Your personal representation of your agency determines for clients the quality of work they can expect from the agency as a whole. The responsibility inherent in your role is significant, so pay very close attention to everything you do. Every detail matters. Embrace and appreciate the power you have to impact client impressions. Keep it top-of-mind at all times and make sure you are forming *positive* client impressions that lead to improving client partnerships.

Create a business-building bridge

Refuse to be a typical agency "order taker" that provides adequate service and grants clients only what they request. Rather, be a passionate and proactive business partner. Create and maintain a strong "business-building bridge" between your agency and your clients. To this end, provide your clients with a steady stream of *unsolicited* proposals that demonstrate how passionate you are about growing their businesses. In doing so, it is critical that you *focus on generating long-term growth for your clients,* not short-term sales for your agency. If your clients' businesses grow as a result of your passionate and proactive leadership, your agency's business will grow in turn.

I can tell you from experience that passionate and proactive client leadership pays dividends. As the chief account officer for the Cincinnati office of Interbrand, an Omnicom global branding agency, I introduced an initiative I dubbed *"Project Proactivity."* The idea behind this initiative was to instill in every member of my large account team how critical it was for them to be passionate and proactive. I articulated and documented clearly a plethora of expectations for my team, but I wanted everyone to know that above all else they needed to demonstrate a passionate and proactive approach to improving client partnerships, on a daily basis. In my estimation, this was the most important thing my team could do to generate success.

Each time a member of my account team forwarded an unsolicited business-building proposal to a client, they filled out for me this simple one-page template to provide a compelling overview of the recommendation:

Account Team Member	
Other Key Contributors *(Identify partners from other departments, if applicable)*	
Brand	
Proposal	
Who *(Client's name/title)*	
What *(Brief description of recommendation)*	
Why *(Business need on which it delivers uniquely for client)*	
Budget Estimate	
Status *(Pending, approved, declined)*	

The key was to capture why it was a good idea for the client (i.e., what client need it met uniquely). I would then post this sheet under the person's name on this public "scorecard" I created outside my office:

This scorecard served three purposes. First, it created friendly competition. Anyone who is aggressive and competitive — which you need to be to succeed as a client leader — wouldn't want blank space under their name; they would want the most sheets. Secondly, this scorecard clearly illustrated the priority of the initiative and ensured on-going focus and effort. Lastly, it encouraged sharing of ideas among the team members. If someone needed ideas to take to their clients, the first place to start was the scorecard to see what inspired insights other members of the team had developed. At P&G we called this "search and re-apply."

In addition to the scorecard, other recognition and monetary incentives were built in to reward those individuals who were the most successful in taking initiative and helping their clients win.

"Project Proactivity" proved to be a significant driver of incremental revenue, accounting for over 10% of the office's revenue base during its first year of implementation. Interbrand has 40 offices around the world. Each year the group chairman and CEO — Chuck Brymer, now president and CEO of DDB Worldwide — chaired "Best Work Awards," a formal recognition program, which consisted of five categories. "Project Proactivity" won the award for the most successful "Business-Building" effort across the global network of offices.

More importantly, the unsolicited feedback from our clients was overwhelmingly positive. They did not see this initiative as an effort to simply sell them more stuff. Rather, they recognized and appreciated our sincere interest in growing their businesses in a strategic and sustainable manner.

These results prove that clients want their agencies to be passionate and proactive business partners — and clients will find money for good ideas. So, if your clients' businesses grow, your agency's business will grow in turn. It is your job to create and maintain this win-win business-building bridge.

Compel partnership-related results

Adopting a model mindset is critically important in the process of improving client partnerships. As outlined in the previous chapters of this first section, a model mindset consists of concentrating on continual self-improvement, an appreciation for your personal power in improving clients' perceptions of your agency, and an external focus on growing your clients' businesses in order to grow your agency's business.

As you adopt this model mindset, it is crucial that you stay focused on the positive results it can and should deliver vis-à-vis your client partnerships. In fact, *you* need to *compel* these results. You need to lead the effort and maintain a powerful and irresistible influence. In particular, you should focus on the following three goals:

1. *Be perceived by your clients as the best external partner who works on their businesses.* In today's world of highly-specialized and integrated communications, most clients engage with several different agencies at the same time. You should want to be seen as the most impressive partner among all the agencies — and it starts with being the most passionate and proactive. Don't simply fill needs and meet expectations. Anticipate needs and exceed expectations. Look to add value in everything you do — both

internally and externally. Consistently and flawlessly execute a proven set of best practices that set you apart from the client leaders in the other agencies.

2. *Constantly improve your clients' perceptions of your agency based on your outstanding representation and leadership.* You have the personal power to create a positive impact on client perceptions. Don't forget it. Embrace it and take advantage of it every day, in everything you do. Work tirelessly to eliminate any and all negative client perceptions of your agency and build momentum behind positive perceptions. In addition to your clients' perceptions that you are the best external partner working on their businesses, you want your agency to be regarded as the best for their businesses. Make this happen.

3. *Become an indispensable business partner.* It's one thing for your clients to like you. It's even better to reach the point where they want you involved in all key projects and meetings. It's ideal, though, when they *need* you involved. When you reach this point in your relationships you have become indispensable to your clients. This is the ultimate proof of partnership. Strive for nothing less.

Once you have firmly adopted a model mindset — including a determination to deliver partnership-related results — you should work on continually developing the quintessential qualities and skills that will help you succeed. This is the focus of the next section.

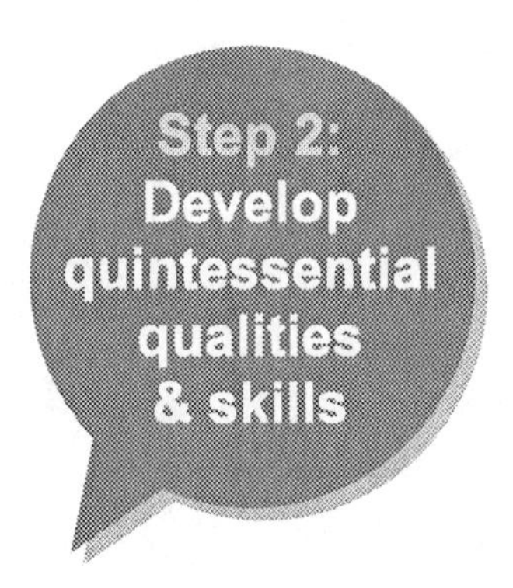

I am often asked, "What does it take to be a good client leader?" A simple enough question with a not-so-simple answer. To be a truly outstanding "face" of an agency and to build truly strong client partnerships requires a plethora of talents. A balance of style and substance. A blend of left- and right-brain thinking. A combination of internal and external influences. A lot.

There is no right or wrong answer to the question. It is very subjective. Anyone who has ever had success as a client leader or a leader of an account team will have his or her own list of qualities and skills — articulated in a personal manner. As mentioned in the introduction, I wrote this book to share my personal perspective and unique points of view.

I believe firmly that success starts with being PASSIONATE and PROACTIVE in how you approach everything. **Along with a model mindset, think of these qualities as your foundation of success.**

In this section I will expand on the importance of being passionate and proactive — then share and discuss a list of other qualities and skills that I believe are essential building blocks of a well-rounded and high-impact partner — a partner on whom your clients can count. This list is not exhaustive. But based on experience, I believe it is a good place to start and focus.

The final section will build on the foundation of this section by providing practical tips for putting these qualities and skills into practice. These tips will then be brought to life with real-world examples of successful implementation that led to improved partnerships.

Be passionate

Renowned philosopher Georg Wilhelm proclaimed, "Nothing great in the world has been accomplished without passion." I couldn't agree more. Without exception I believe that you cannot maximize your potential in a particular pursuit if you don't love what you are doing. If you don't take tremendous pride in your effort and results. If you don't wake up every morning raring to go. If you don't find yourself thinking constantly about the future and what's next.

Having passion is critical. *Exhibiting* your passion is just as important. Doing so instills your excitement in other people. When this happens, when you motivate and persuade others through genuine enthusiasm, anything is possible. As a client leader, you can't expect your clients to be excited about your agency or its work if you're not animated and excited about it. Remember, you are the face of the agency. If you are passionate, excited, energetic and inspiring, your clients will perceive your agency in the same manner.

This is particularly true in meetings with new clients who likely have not yet formed an opinion. First impressions make lasting impressions. Nothing beats clients walking away from an initial meeting with you and your agency thinking, "Wow, those people love what they do!" Clients will want you doing it for *them*. They recognize that agencies do their best work when inspired, excited and passionate. These traits serve as magnets for clients.

I often find that client leaders — particularly junior ones — may be passionate about their role, but at the same time feel like they have to be overly-professional in client meetings. This is especially true in new business pitches. As a result, they can come across as too stiff, serious, disengaged, or simply boring and uninspiring.

Don't get me wrong; you need to be professional in order to garner trust and respect. But, don't be afraid to let your passion flow. When presenting, don't stand in a stationary position with your hands by your side. Walk around. Exude energy. Be animated. Smile. Laugh. Project your voice without yelling. Say you love what you do, with every action. Say how much you want to work with the clients. Say how much you love their brands or businesses. Do it with sincerity and conviction by looking the clients in the eyes when you say it.

The power of this approach never ceases to amaze me. It's engaging. It makes clients want to hear what else you have to say. To want to work with you. To entrust you with their "babies." To invite you to be their strategic partner. Passion is powerful.

Be proactive

Outstanding client leaders don't wait for their clients or managers to provide direction, make recommendations, or ask for something. They are not followers; they are leaders. They are not passive; they are aggressive. They are not complacent; they are restless. They are action-oriented go-getters who are hell-bent on making things happen. Said simply, they are proactive.

Being proactive is a great way to demonstrate your passion. Learn as much as you can about your clients' businesses, industries and competitors. What are their short- and long-term objectives and strategies? What are they doing well? Where do they need to improve? What are their competitors up to? And most importantly, what keeps your clients up at night?

In addition to becoming an expert on your clients' businesses you need to have a very firm handle on your agency's business. What services does your agency provide and what unique value do they offer?

Once you understand your clients' needs and your agency's services, take the initiative in finding ways to marry the two. Don't wait for your clients to indicate a problem or opportunity and ask if your agency can help. Beat them to the punch. Provide your clients with a steady stream of *unsolicited* proposals that demonstrate how passionate you are about growing their businesses. Your clients won't approve every proposal. But, if your proposals are strategically sound and thoughtful, your clients will appreciate every one.

Be positive

Being a client leader is often a thankless job. In the fast-paced environment in which you work you'll find that clients don't have time to provide a great dealt of unsolicited feedback. If and when they do, more often than not it's critical, not positive. Do a great job on something and you might receive a "thanks" at best. Screw something up and trust me, you'll hear about it in excruciating detail. Certainly there are exceptions. But in general, clients tend to be tough and demanding. And that's to be expected. They are under tremendous pressure from their management and looking to you to make sure they deliver results.

To succeed and be happy you can't be deterred by the pressure. You cannot become cynical, negative or doubtful. You must have thick skin and you must remain positive. Negativity is carcinogenic. Your clients will see it and begin to lose confidence and respect in you. They are counting on you. Nothing less than a consistently strong "can do" spirit will suffice.

This is why being passionate about what you're doing is so important. You should be in this position because you love what you do. Keeping this in mind at all times will help you to maintain a positive outlook. Your passion will perpetuate a positive predisposition.

Be buttoned up

Another way to gain clients' confidence is to be buttoned up and organized. Remember, clients are counting on you. They have placed a ton of faith in you. You can't appear out of control. You can't constantly show up late to meetings. You can't appear unable to manage your calendar. You can't lose important documents. You can't keep asking the same questions over and over again. You can't miss deadlines. You can't forget things — even the smallest of details. You must *be* and *look* 100% buttoned up — and it has to look effortless.

I highly encourage you to find and stick to an organizational system and set of tools that work for you. Experiment with a few options until you find some that are foolproof; that ensure nothing falls through the cracks. That manage every complex detail of your job. That keep all important information at your fingertips. Phone numbers. E-mail addresses. Action items. Deadlines.

It takes time to become and stay organized. But, this time is more than offset by the time it will ultimately save. You won't waste time looking for lost items, putting out fires created by missed deadlines, or explaining to a client why you missed an important meeting.

Remember, you are the face of the agency. Everything you do — no matter how big or small — reflects upon your agency and impacts your clients' perceptions of it. The slightest miss on your behalf can have a significant impact on your client partnerships. And your agency tenure.

Be consultative

An agency "order taker" traffics work back and forth between clients and the agency. Clients receive what clients request. At best. If the clients don't feel that the work meets expectations, they request changes. The order taker takes the work and the client-directed changes back to the agency for the internal team to review and address. The order taker then brings the revised work back to the clients for a second review. If the clients are not happy, it's back to the agency with more changes. And so the vicious cycle continues. Order takers don't add value. And they most certainly don't build client partnerships. They approach their roles with a service orientation, not a consultative orientation.

To end or avoid this vicious cycle you need to stay ahead of your clients. You need to lead your clients' thinking, not react to it. You need to provide proactive advice. Ideas. Counsel. Direction. Effective client leaders are, in fact, leaders. Not reactive order takers.

If you ask clients what they want, they will undoubtedly say, "I'll know it when I see it." I have heard this disconcerting statement countless times in my career. Heck, I may have even said it when I was a brand manager at the beginning of my career! It is not the client's fault. Without any leadership and consultation from the agency as to what the agency can and should do, clients are forced to try and tell the agency what it is they need from them. This isn't good for anyone. Work will be kicked off without a truly clear concept, objective or direction. Inevitably, the delivery of the work — timing, budget and quality — will suffer, because the clients will keep making subjective changes in lieu of a clear, conceptual framework and consultation from the agency.

Be a consultant. Ask questions. Probe deeply. Really listen to your clients. Peel away the surface issues and dive down to the real problems your clients face. Tell them what you think. State your opinion. Be decisive. Offer ideas. Share "game changing" solutions. Clients want thought leaders, new ideas and people who speak their minds. They do not want "yes-men," or people who will back down from a true discussion on their businesses in an effort to satiate them. Know your subject matter and own your thoughts (and the rationale behind them). Clients will truly appreciate your passion and drive — even if your ideas run counter to their line of thinking.

Before your agency initiates any work, make sure your team has a clear, concise and compelling project brief. Don't hope or expect your clients will create it. Take the initiative to draft the brief and share it with your clients for input and approval. Lead the strategic thinking. Define the project scope. Articulate the ideal end goal and key interim milestones to achieve it. Be a consultant, not an order taker.

If your ideas ultimately create value for your clients, as they should, don't be bashful. Make sure your clients are fully aware of the value they received. Document it in a success story and share it with them. Then, offer to share it with their management to help your clients look like superstars.

If your clients want your agency to do something that doesn't make sense and/or doesn't address the real problem, tell them. For their sake. Never say "no." But don't be afraid to disagree tactfully and offer alternative suggestions. Do it with confidence and conviction, but also with empathy. Clients tend to resist and/or become defensive rather than readily acknowledge the real problem (especially if they created it). You can push hard as long as you position carefully.

Know when to back down. Remember, it's about battles and wars. You don't need to win all of the former to prevail in the latter. Show your clients that you're smart, but tactful. That you think, not just react. That you're empathetic. That you're passionate and proactive. That you have great ideas for their businesses. That you want their businesses to succeed. That you are a consultative partner.

Be confident

Your clients are counting on you. They need to deliver results and they need your help. You are their key partner. In order to count on you, clients count on your confidence. You must be confident — and you must show it. Clients can smell fear. Don't let them.

The best way to demonstrate confidence is to be comfortable. Be comfortable in your understanding of your clients. Be comfortable in what your agency does. Be comfortable in what you do. If you know your stuff cold, you will have a very strong confidence level — and it will show. In the way you carry yourself. In the way you engage with clients. In the way you present your agency's work. Your clients will sense your confidence and be drawn to you like a magnet. They will want you to be their partner because they will know you can help them deliver results. Your confidence will boost their confidence.

Be strategic

A daily demonstration of passion and initiative can be very impressive. Unsolicited business-building proposals are a great way to show your clients how excited you are to help them succeed. But in order to avoid looking like a used-car salesman you need to be strategic.

This is an area ripe with opportunity to shine, because among the majority of clients it is a key perceived shortcoming. Most clients think their agency representatives are spread too thinly and as a result, don't have enough time to develop a strategic understanding of their businesses. If you can demonstrate successfully to clients that you are fully engaged and that you have sound strategic ideas for their businesses, you will quickly shatter their pre-conceived notions and rise above the status quo.

At its core a strategy is a choice. So, to be strategic you have to be selective. To achieve an objective you need to assess all your possibilities and identify only a manageable number of options that will have the most impact. A strategy requires sacrifice. This is how your clients manage their businesses and it's how you should, too.

In order to successfully sell new business-building proposals, the first thing you need to do is gain an understanding of key client dynamics. How are your clients evaluated? What is on their work & development plans? How do they go about securing approval from their management for new proposals? What are their company's criteria for reviewing commercial innovation ideas? When is the best time to submit proposals? It's great to share unsolicited strategic proposals with your clients, but if you do so two weeks after their annual budget planning process is complete, your chance of success is drastically reduced.

Once you understand these critically-important client dynamics, set out to develop and share with them your carefully thought-through proposals that truly make sense for their businesses. But you can't sell a solution until you strategically assess the situation and simplify the problem or opportunity. To do this, you must truly know their businesses, industries and competitors. And you need to really understand the unique benefits of what your agency offers. Then, look for ways to strategically marry what your agency can do with what your clients need.

Once you have done this, work hard to develop a compelling but simple proposition for your clients. If your proposition is too complex, and thus takes too much work on your clients' behalf to understand it, you will compromise the potential of what may be a big idea.

Share compelling ideas with your clients, but don't talk price. First, make your clients excited about the possibilities. Then, work with them to determine the value.

Lastly, you must focus on quality, not quantity. If your clients perceive your proactive efforts as just a constant attempt to sell them everything your agency offers — regardless of how relevant it may be — your good intentions will go awry. Focus on the clients, not the sale. You must be selective. You must be strategic.

Be a leader

As noted several times already (though it can never be stated enough) clients are counting on you to help them deliver results. You are their partner and key point of contact with the agency.

So, clients need to see that you are in charge and in control. Do you have a vision for how to manage your clients' businesses? Have you rallied the rest of your agency team — creatives, planners, analysts, management — in support of this vision? Does the team listen to you, demonstrate respect and respond to you as the representative of the clients? Is the team inspired by you? Persuaded by you? *Do your clients see it?* Ask yourself these tough questions and be tough with your answers. If you can honestly answer "yes" to them, then you are well on your way as a leader that your agency and your clients need.

To go beyond "order taker" you must be able to make things happen — quickly and effectively. Not all clients will secure the benefit of your agency's "A-Team." If your clients do, not all of them are necessarily going to obtain the best work from this top talent. Not all clients receive a significant amount of your management's precious time. It is your job to be a strong leader and make sure your clients realize more than their fair share of your agency's resources, talent and thinking, to build their businesses. To do this, you need to be aggressive. You need to be visionary. You need to be inspiring. You need to be persuasive. You need to be a champion. You need to be unwavering and relentless. Said simply, you need to be a leader.

Be a relationship builder

The true definition of a "relationship" is a fundamentally misunderstood concept in the agency world. A true client relationship is not defined by your clients liking you. Or going to ball games. Or nice lunches. Or drinks after focus groups. Or having fun reviewing creative work together. Don't get me wrong; having a solid personal relationship is important. But, you ultimately have to evolve it into a strong professional relationship. One built on trust. Respect. Need. You need your clients to need you. To view you as an indispensable business partner.

Like any relationship, you must work at it. And while it takes two, you should approach it with the attitude that you have the lion's share of work. It is not 50/50. You need to earn your clients' respect and trust — they don't necessarily have to earn yours.

To earn their respect and trust, start by showing your passion. Let your clients see it in your eyes. Then, demonstrate initiative as quickly in the relationship-building process as possible. The sooner you come to your clients with strategic, thoughtful and well articulated business-building ideas, the sooner you will exceed their expectations and the less likely they will see you as a stereotypical agency order taker. And the sooner you will garner respect.

To turn respect into unwavering trust, it is critical that your proposals focus on generating long-term growth for your clients, not short-term sales for your agency. You need to make what you have to offer clear to your clients, but you can't stop there. You also must make it very clear how your proposals are in your clients' best interest, not yours. Articulate clearly the value your clients can expect to derive from what you offer.

Once your clients are excited about your ideas, follow-through is critical. Deliver what you promised — and more — on time and on budget (if not ahead of schedule and under budget). This will continue to build your clients' level of respect and trust for you.

When your client's respect and trust is established, you earn the right to take more risks on their behalf. You earn the right to be wrong. You earn the right to speak more freely and openly about what you believe, because your clients will know you have their best interests in mind. You earn the ability to be a better consultant, because you will have built a better client relationship.

Be a great communicator

Regardless of the type of agency for which you work, you are ultimately in the communications business. Your agency serves to help clients communicate successfully with their customers, consumers and constituents. So if you are going to be the face of a communications company, you must be a great communicator.

A good communicator is complex. But I have found that if you focus on the following sequence, you will be well on your way: be clear, be concise, be passionate, be persuasive — then be gone. This applies to all forms of verbal and written communication — from formal presentations to brief e-mails.

Clients should understand what you are saying and they must be moved by it. To ensure comprehension of what you are saying, you have to be crystal clear and concise. Most clients are hard-driving type-A personalities, with the attention span of a gnat. They have a million things going on and they are in a perpetual state of multi-tasking. You must attain their attention and maintain it long enough to make your point. To get their attention, get to the "What's in it for me?" as quickly as possible. Don't make clients work for it or wait to hear it.

To hold their attention, be passionate and persuasive. If you are excited about an idea, you are much more likely to create excitement in them. If they are excited, they will pause long enough to hear more. But they won't engage forever. Make your point powerfully and quickly. Then, be gone. Don't waste your clients' time.

And whatever you do, don't make the mistake of "un-selling" your idea by saying something that concerns your clients and/or allows time for their change of mind. If they buy the idea, stop talking. Stop selling. You have reached a successful end point. Continuing to engage clients now can't help any more. It can only cause harm. Stop the presentation. Zip up the portfolio. Say "thank you." If clients understand and buy your idea — often indicated by clients saying "got it!" — your job is done. A great communicator knows when to stop communicating.

Be a great listener

For most agency people, talking comes quite naturally. Listening — *truly listening* — is the hard part. We usually pretend we are listening. But let's be honest. More often than not we are actually thinking about what we are going to say next and just waiting for the slightest pause in the conversation to say it.

Active listening is critical for two reasons: 1) Clients want to be heard; and 2) You need to really hear them if you are going to help them. You need to hear what they say and what they *don't* say. Ask numerous questions to inspire clients' talking and sharing as much as possible — especially in the early stages of a new relationship or project. Ultimately, you will need to provide your point of view if you are going to be seen as a consultative partner. But, listen to what clients think first. They will feel like they have been heard and you will undoubtedly benefit from what they say. Leverage their comments as a context for framing and supporting your point of view.

Listening is often not enough. You need to learn to *understand* what clients really *mean* by what they say. For example, "This is a great range of work," doesn't necessarily mean, "Wow, you have explored options I never would have thought of." Instead, it usually means that the clients have nothing positive to say and that's the closest they could come to a compliment.

While it is important to be a good listener, it is even more important that your clients know you are listening. Demonstrate it by taking notes. Nodding. Restating what they said as a segue to what you are waiting to say. And again, ask questions. Lots of questions. Questions show you care. They show you are curious. They show you are passionate. They show you are listening. And if you listen to your clients they will listen to you.

Be curious

As noted in the previous chapter, asking questions shows you are curious.

Be curious about your clients. What are their personal objectives? Career aspirations? What keeps them up at night? What more can you do to help them?

Be curious about their businesses and industries. What are the latest trends? What's happening in related industries? What motivates shoppers and consumers? Where's the white space of unmet needs?

Be curious about their competitors. Try their products and services. What's working for them? What are their weaknesses and, thus, potential points of vulnerability? What are the perceptions of their consumers?

If you find yourself at a loss for providing good input in a meeting, ask a good question. Sometimes a really smart question can add more value than a really smart statement. Your curiosity will make others curious. It can take the meeting in a new and better direction.

Curiosity shows you care. Caring shows you are a good partner. Clients love curious agency partners.

Be accountable

The best way to prove to your clients that they can count on you is to behave in a consistently accountable manner. I recognize that this is not a very profound statement. But every day I see client leaders take action that undermines their accountability. And so often the mistakes are small and easily avoidable. Remember, *everything* you do — however big or small — impacts clients' perceptions of you and your agency.

Proving your accountability is rather simple: pay attention to basic fundamentals. Deliver on your promises. Meet or ideally, exceed, expectations. Don't miss deadlines. Ever. Don't surprise clients with budget overages. Ever. If you don't think your agency's work is prepared enough to show your clients yet, say so. If you make a mistake, say so. Admitting it and fixing it will build your credibility. Tying to cover it up will kill your credibility.

If you hold yourself accountable, clients will continue to count on you. If they have to hold you accountable, you can count on them losing confidence.

Be fun

I haven't met a client yet that doesn't think agencies are more fun than the company for which they work. The diversity of the people and the creative nature of the work generate fun and excitement. As such, clients love hanging out with their agency teams — especially at the agency offices, which are almost without exception, much cooler.

Hanging out and having fun with clients is very important for a couple of reasons.

- *It's important that clients like you.* As I have said previously, this is not the ultimate measurement of a solid client partnership. But, it is a good step in the right direction. If clients are going to like you, they have to come to know you. And you need to know them. Take them to lunch. Go to a ball game. Anything that is conducive to a meaningful level of fun and conversation. Your agency undoubtedly has season tickets to several arts and sporting events. Take advantage of them and take your clients. When you go, don't talk work. Talk family, sports, other interests … *anything* but work (except politics and religion!).

- *Better relationships lead to better work.* When team members like one another and have fun together, they

> spend more time together. They communicate better. They are more honest with one another. More comfortable with one another. More willing to challenge one another. More willing to support one another. More willing to take risks together. And as a result, much more likely to create better work together.

Have fun with your clients. You'll create better work and stronger partnerships.

Be consistent

Once you develop all of the previously-mentioned qualities and skills, you need to focus on displaying them in a consistent manner. Every day. In everything you do.

Clients are counting on you every day—you need to show them *every day* that they can. Show the same passion. The same proactive nature. The same positive predisposition. The same compelling confidence. The same buttoned-up dependability and accountability. The same consultative and strategic thinking. The same leadership that makes things happen. The same effective communication and listening skills. The same inquisitive curiosity. The same fun personality. Said simply, you need to be the same great partner on whom your clients count — every day in every way.

Be yourself

There are definitely many qualities and skills that are essential to being an effective client leader. And as mentioned a few times already, the list that has been provided in this section of *Tell Your Clients Where to Go!* is by no means exhaustive. There are several factors to consider and remember. It's hard. So, it's easy to forget the most important thing: be yourself.

The last thing you want to do is appear insincere or artificial. As in any relationship, you succeed by letting your unique personality shine through. People don't warm up to a perfectly honed and balanced set of skills and qualities; people warm up to other people. Be human.

A big part of being human is *not* being perfect. And that's okay. In fact, it can be endearing. If you adopt the mindset that you are the face of the agency — and therefore everything you do impacts your clients' perceptions of it — this can be a daunting and difficult balancing act.

How can you professionally represent your agency and not be perfect all the time? Simple. Be yourself. Be proud of who you are. Showcase your unique personality. Admit mistakes in a contrite and honest fashion. Genuinely laugh at your imperfections. Readily accept the imperfections of others. You can't be perfect. You should be yourself. Focus on this first and everything else will come much more easily and naturally.

It takes plenty to be a great partner to your clients. You can never become complacent. You need to work constantly on improving your performance in order to improve your client partnerships. This starts with adopting a model mindset that includes a determination to deliver partnership-related results. Then, you need to develop several important qualities and skills — focusing on passionate and proactive client leadership as a foundation on which to build.

A great way to continually develop the quintessential qualities and skills outlined in this past section is to put them into practice and apply them every day. The following and final section offers practical how-to advice and tips.

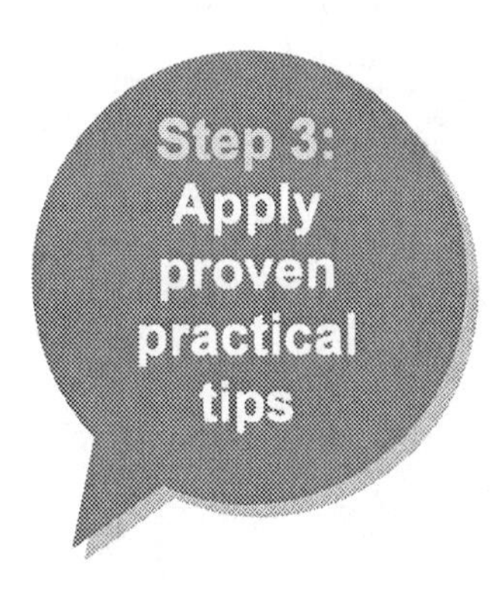

There are a few good books focused on how to lead clients and build client partnerships. They each offer a uniquely valuable perspective. Since there is no definitive authority, you can and should benefit from a broad range of perspectives that appeal to you. These books, however, fall short in offering specific and actionable tips that can be implemented, in order to practice the general fundamentals the books preach.

This final section of *Tell Your Clients Where to Go!* offers advice that is practical, important and prioritized. The advice is brought to life with tips for applying it and — where appropriate — personal examples of how doing so positively impacted actual client partnerships. These examples are masked or modified as necessary to appropriately protect confidential client work and information.

I hope you find these tips and examples helpful. Throughout my career I have used them to successfully lead, manage and coach client leaders, other client-facing staff members, *and clients*. Refer to these tips often and apply them as much as possible.

Exceed expectations every day

Meeting your clients' expectations will not separate you from the horde of "order takers" out there. You must find ways to *exceed* expectations. Do this constantly. Never stop looking. There is no better way to show your clients you care and that you are a leader on which they can count.

Practical tips:

- *Find a way to pleasantly surprise at least one client a day with something they were not expecting.* This can be something complex like a significant new business-building proposal. Or, it can be something quite simple like a copy of a relevant industry article, with a cover note offering some perspective. Maybe it is a new competitive product you found while shopping. Or an ad for a completely unrelated item that inspired an idea for your clients' businesses. Or a deliverable delivered one day early. Or a simple e-mail to follow up on something. It could be anything, as long as it is relevant and adds value in some way.

  The key is to demonstrate to your clients that you are passionate about their businesses and constantly seeking new ways to help them grow. Ask yourself every day before leaving work if you have surprised at least one client with something they were not expecting. Don't leave until you are satisfied that you have.

- *Look for ways to help your clients look good.* If they look good, you and your agency look good. Send their managers complimentary notes about them (when warranted). Or query their administrative assistants and find out what important meetings they have coming up with their management. Then, offer to help them prepare. Maybe they need some engaging visuals aids, which agencies are much better at creating than clients. Maybe they need some samples of your agency's work, which you certainly want them showing their management. It's worth the time to prepare.

- *Don't just focus on senior-level clients; go out of your way to impress junior clients, as well.* They will really appreciate it and remember it. And before you know it, they will be senior clients with more authority. If you build a strong partnership with them early on in their careers by exceeding their expectations, they will want to keep you close as they rise up the ranks. Every day I see experienced agency leaders scoff at junior clients. This may not matter in the present time, but the short-sightedness will prove problematic down the road.

Personal example:
Pleasantly surprising a client with something they were not expecting.

A few years ago I enthusiastically offered my agency's pro-bono help to the National Underground Railroad Freedom Center. I am very passionate about the notion that businesses should give back to their communities. It's the right thing to do. However, since agencies operate with limited resources, they need to be fiscally responsible and ensure that pro-bono work offers some benefit to their own businesses. In this case, the Freedom Center offered a highly visible forum for our work. And the CEO at the time was John E. Pepper — the former chairman and CEO of Procter & Gamble, and currently the chairman of the board of the Walt Disney Company. Our biggest client was P&G, so a positive endorsement of our work from Mr. Pepper would have been of great value. This was a perfect win-win engagement.

The Freedom Center needed some brand positioning help. They have a wonderfully inspirational mission to reveal stories about freedom's heroes, from the era of the Underground Railroad to contemporary times, challenging and inspiring everyone to take courageous steps for freedom today. However, most people who had never been to the museum expected it to focus simply on slavery and its subsequent abolishment.

In partnership with Mr. Pepper and his great team, we set out to change that false perception — and we did. My agency developed a simple yet powerful image of two arms in a locked embrace, accompanied by the simple line: "Join the Journey." In this case, it was a black man's arm locked with a white man's arm. But, the visual had the flexibility to be campaign-able. For the 9/11 exhibit, it could be a fireman's arm locked with a baby's arm. It could be the arms of an old woman and a young woman. It could be any two arms. The idea was simple: there has been, there is, and there will continue to be a fight for various kinds of freedom — so come see what it's all about and how you can become involved. A very inspiring and mind-opening message with an overt call-to-action.

When we first presented this image to Mr. Pepper, his eyes lit up and he smiled. He proceeded to offer plenty of very positive feedback, including the statement, "[That image] is the sculpture I have always dreamed of commissioning." Obviously, he was pleased with our work.

Since this was the deliverable we committed to produce, our work was basically done. We could have simply finished the production work, accepted their appreciation, and moved on to our paying clients. There was more we could do, though, and I felt that it was the right thing to offer more pro-bono help.

Driving back to the agency with my two colleagues I couldn't get Mr. Pepper's quote about the sculpture out of my head. When he said it in the meeting, it was in the middle of excited feedback. So most people in the room did not make much of it; but it resonated with me, as I was listening intently to all of Mr. Pepper's feedback. When we arrived back at the agency I said to my colleagues, "You know what? We should commission the sculpture that Mr. Pepper said he always dreamed of!"

So we did. We found a sculptress and arranged to have her sketch a prototype. In addition, I decided our agency should donate a significant portion of the funds necessary to create the sculpture.

We met again with Mr. Pepper and his team about two weeks later. The intended purpose of this follow-up meeting was simply to share detailed production plans for the work to which we had already committed.

When the meeting was near ending, I said, "Hang on, we have something else." Mr. Pepper looked surprised, but said, "Okay." I proceeded to pull out of the portfolio a comical presentation board. Although he is a very serious businessman, Mr. Pepper is a gregarious person with a wonderful sense of humor. So we decided to have a little fun. The board contained a picture of him eating Pringles (a P&G brand). We "Photoshop'ed" Mickey Mouse ears on him, since he was just appointed to the post of Walt Disney Company chairman. We also included his quote about our visual of the two arms in a locked embrace.

The presentation board:

I asked Mr. Pepper if he remembered saying this in our last meeting. He said he did. I responded by saying, "Great … because we did, in fact, commission it!" The look of surprise on his face was priceless.

We proceeded to reveal the artistic renderings of the sculpture, which was followed with a large mock-up of the check — picture the big check presented to winners of golf tournaments — that we wanted to donate to help pay for the sculpture. With a look of astonishment on his face, he said, "What's next? Are you going to tell me the sculpture is already done and in the lobby downstairs?" Clearly, we exceeded his expectations.

Partnership impact:

We received a formal letter from Mr. Pepper a few days after our meeting (a copy can be found on page 58). In the very thoughtful and gracious letter Mr. Pepper stated, "I am really excited about the path that we have drawn going forward.

You are all very patient with us as we work our way toward the long-term positioning we need. I am very optimistic we will find a way … to something great. To add to that, your thoughtfulness in developing the design for the sculpture I've long dreamed of, then to find a sculptress who could carry out the work, then to donate $5,000 for its execution … that is truly over the top."

As I mentioned before, our biggest client was P&G. So, needless to say, we derived significant mileage out of this wonderful note from Mr. Pepper, who is idolized by current and former P&G'ers — as he should be; he is an amazing person.

By listening closely to what he said and exceeding his expectations with passion and initiative, we improved our partnership with him, and our largest client. And we did the right thing for the community. It was a success all around.

The letter from Mr. Pepper:

John E. Pepper
Chief Executive Officer

July 21, 2006

Mr. Todd Sebastian

Dear Todd,

These few words won't begin to convey my gratitude to all that you, Tara and Anita brought to us in our meeting yesterday.

I am really excited about the path that we have drawn going forward. You are all very patient with us as we work our way toward the long-term positioning we need. I am very optimistic we will find a way . . . to something great.

To add to that, your thoughtfulness in developing the design for that sculpture I've long dreamed of, then to find a sculptress who could carry out the work, and then to donate $5,000 for its execution . . . that is truly over the top. I can't wait to see it executed. And, before that, to have the chance to meet the person who will do it.

I look forward to continuing to work with you. Please know that you all have given us an enormous lift as we pursue this journey to make the Freedom Center all it can be.

Warm regards,

John E. Pepper

cc: Greg Landsman

JEP:mr
Todd Sebastian

50 East Freedom Way • Cincinnati, OH 45202 • Tel: 513.333.7545 • Fax: 513-733-7712 • Email: [illegible]

Personal example:
Helping a client look good.

Providing unsolicited feedback can be very powerful. And feedback should go both ways in any relationship. Client relationships are no exception. So, when warranted, I often provide clients — and/or their managers — with unsolicited feedback.

A while back I began to develop what is now a very strong relationship with an outstanding P&G brand manager. She had some issues with our agency. To her credit, she expressed her concerns in a very forthright, transparent and productive manner. Unlike some clients who simply complain about an agency behind its back, she wanted us to know about the issues directly and grant us a chance to address them. Moreover, she offered to roll up her sleeves and help.

My team very much appreciated her partnership-oriented behavior, so I sent what I thought was a very simple note of acknowledgement and gratitude to her manager. I do this type of thing often, but only when it is truly warranted. In this particular case, it was extremely warranted. She is an outstanding person and client partner.

Subsequently, my client had a meeting with her manager and reported back to me in an e-mail, "In my meeting with (my manager) this week when we were talking about all the work I was doing that she did not know about she said, 'The first time I realized you were doing excellent work was when I received that note from Todd.' So, nothing really has broken through to her to this point except your note, which meant a lot and I guess put me on her radar screen. Actually, she has sent me many notes of accolades but she does not remember ... the one thing sticking in her mind is your note. So, regardless of how much she forgets, I appreciate that your note meant so much to her, likely because she respects you so much."

Partnership impact:

The few minutes it took for me to acknowledge my client's great work to her manager — justifiably so — proved to have a very positive impact on her relationship with her manager. And it created a very strong bond between us, based on mutual respect. Often something this simple, when done with genuine passion, can be the catalyst to a strong client partnership.

Personal example:
Providing unexpected business-building consultation.

Our agency had developed a significantly renewed visual identity for a struggling brand. Overall, the objective was to contemporize the brand and differentiate it versus its primary competitor, which was evolving its executional equities and beginning to encroach on the look and feel of the brand on which we were working. This brand has a fairly complicated mechanism of action. As such, a key component of our overall re-branding effort focused on a visual device that could explain simply and clearly the mechanism of action, to improve shopper and consumer understanding and create a compelling point of competitive differentiation.

After developing a unique new visual identity for the brand, we created branding guidelines for other agencies to leverage in order to maintain brand consistency across various media. In the next step we developed new packaging that adhered to the new guidelines and met the communication goals for the complicated mechanism of action. Our agency team was very proud of, and passionate about, the work.

Shortly after we completed this project I saw a 30-second television spot for the brand. The advertising agency responsible for the spot did a fairly good job of leveraging the new visual identity we created. However, the visual device for communicating the mechanism of action was alarmingly different than the one our agency created and utilized on the back of the brand's new packaging.

Our team pointed out this branding inconsistency to the brand manager and offered our help in working with the advertising agency to resolve it. We made it clear that we would do this solely because we have so much passion for the brand and the work we just completed for it. We were not looking for incremental revenue. We indicated that we simply noticed — and wanted to bring to her attention — an opportunity to improve the consistency of her branding communications. And as her branding consultants, we naturally wanted to offer some suggestions in this effort.

To that end I requested some spec work from our graphic designers to illustrate how our visual device can and should be leveraged in advertising. I believe strongly in the power of "Show me, don't tell me." A simple explanation would have conveyed the idea to my client. But I knew it would be much more powerful to go the extra step, develop the spec work and *show* her. This enabled us to create much more excitement in her, about the idea. We also used this spec work to consult with the advertising agency to help ensure their work consistently leveraged the brand's new visual identity platform.

Partnership impact:

The brand manager truly appreciated the unsolicited offer to help — particularly since she recognized it was not based on an attempt to simply generate more revenue for our agency. We demonstrated our passion in growing her business, not ours. In her reply she noted, "Thanks very much for your note and the proactive work on behalf of (my brand). I agree completely with your POV and look forward to the work!"

Personal example:
Significantly exceeding a client's request.

An important client of mine was tapped to serve as co-chair for the Greater Cincinnati roll-out of the Network of Executive Women. This is a national organization dedicated to attracting, retaining and advancing women in the retail and consumer products industry through education, leadership and business development.

Given the prominence of the Network of Executive Women, this was a highly-visible opportunity for my client to demonstrate her tremendous leadership skills. Since this client leaned on me often for partnership help, she asked me to serve on her leadership team for this effort. Naturally, I agreed.

As our kick-off event neared, my client also leaned on me for help in areas that fell outside of my identified team responsibilities, because she trusted my ability to deliver. We were expecting approximately 300 attendees; and we had secured the CEO of Kroger, my client's customer, to deliver the keynote address. So my client was determined to make this event as successful as possible.

The day before the event my client forwarded the speech and PowerPoint presentation to me that she had intended to use during her opening remarks. She simply wanted me to add a few specific pieces of information. I reviewed the materials and quickly realized there was more value that could be added, beyond what she requested, and offered to re-create her entire presentation to make it more simple and engaging. Since I was scheduled to attend an all-day meeting, however, I explained it would not be possible to work on it until the evening — so she wouldn't have much time to review and approve my changes. She replied, "Absolutely. Thank you. If this doesn't show how much I trust you, nothing does!"

Partnership Impact:

I worked long into the evening revising my client's presentation. Seeing her new presentation for the first time at a rather late hour, she responded, "Absolutely perfect. I can't tell you how much I appreciate you taking the time to help me with this … it has been a very stressful couple of weeks and I'm actually quite nervous about tomorrow. This has taken a ton of pressure off — I owe you one!"

Stay in constant contact with clients

In order to lead your clients and build productive partnerships with them, you need to spend a significant amount of time with them. So constantly seek ways to increase your frequency of contact with your key clients.

Practical tips:

- *Schedule routine breakfast, lunch, or coffee meetings.* Don't just let them happen sporadically and randomly. And don't wait for your clients to make the suggestion. You need to take the lead on making this happen.

- *Close every client meeting with a recommendation to meet again soon to either continue discussion of the same topic or suggest a new one.* Never let your client relationships fall into a hiatus. It is imperative to be in frequent contact with your clients if you are going to be their indispensable consultant.

- *Walk the halls of your clients' buildings to maintain a presence and generate impromptu conversations.* If you have a few non-consecutive meetings at their headquarters, remain there in between sessions — even if your agency is located nearby. The more your clients see you, the more they will share with you.

And the more they will feel you are part of their team.

To be clear, clients want to see you. I once received a client note complaining that my account team was not visible enough, indicating, "You guys are two blocks away. I should see you here all the time." This was a reminder that client leaders should have a consistent presence, even without having scheduled meetings. Just roam the halls. This is the best way to build relationships. E-mailing is so impersonal and can lead to issues, because messages are open to interpretation. Live conversations are much more productive, efficient and effective.

Personal example:
Creating a formal initiative to increase client contact.

One fairly new relationship my agency was growing with a client had not yet built up enough understanding and trust, making it somewhat sub-optimal. I had begun to build a very strong bond with a key individual on the client side, but she and her team members were still somewhat unsure about other facets of my agency, to which she referred as "black holes."

Recognizing that we had similar issues with other clients, I successfully recommended to my CEO that we implement a "Client in Residence" program — starting with this particular person from the client company. For 13 weeks she spent one day per week working in our office. While she was here, we treated her as if she was part of our internal team. She was in all of our meetings, formal planning sessions, and impromptu conversations. During this time the client gained a much better understanding of, and appreciation for, our challenges, capabilities, approaches and work. She also came to know our team on a much stronger personal and professional level.

Partnership impact:

This initiative to increase client contact knocked down barriers dramatically and brought understanding and clarity to the "black holes." During a routine evaluation of the program the client noted, "Today went great. I know we're only 2 weeks into my 13 week stint, but I really think we should consider extending this pilot together a little longer. We're just getting at the tip of the iceberg here."

Following her 13-week on-site assignment, she invited me to do the same at her office. Needless to say, I agreed. It was a wonderful opportunity. This reciprocation in deep-dive learning and sharing led to significant improvements in the relationship between our two companies.

Keep current on clients

Stay up-to-date on your clients' businesses. Be inquisitive. Try to learn and know as much about the businesses as your clients do — if not more. Knowledge is a critical foundation to being an effective leader and consultant.

Practical tips:

- *Scan your clients' websites a few times a week.* Most clients update their sites routinely. In particular, review the "news" page for press releases. Since not every press release makes its way into an actual media story, this is a great way to discover obscure news and information about your clients.

- *Subscribe to and read trade publications from the industries in which your clients operate.* Come to know their industries as well as they do. Show interest in all aspects of their businesses — not only the aspects that relate directly to your agency's work.

- *Add automatic updates to your web browser home page and review every morning.* These updates should include general industry and client information (including stock prices), as well as updates specific to the product categories and brands you manage.

- *Review your clients' annual reports in detail*. Beyond the helpful financial information, there is no better source for gaining a thorough understanding of your clients' business objectives, strategies and plans. This will provide a very accurate and up-to-date understanding of the issues that keep your clients up at night.

- *Conduct regular store checks*. You need to stay in touch with industry and competitive activity and the perceptions of shoppers and consumers. If your client is in the consumer packaged goods industry, visit retail stores often. Do your family's grocery shopping every week. If your client is in a service industry, engage in the service as a customer. Gain a first-hand understanding of the service experience.

Personal example:
Showing interest in, and knowledge of, all aspects of a client's business.

It is important to show interest in all aspects of your clients' businesses, not just the parts on which you and your agency work. Send your clients information and ideas that you think will be of interest to them, even if there is no potential of generating incremental assignments immediately for your agency. The lack of self-serving benefits to your actions will demonstrate that you are a good partner who truly cares about your clients. And this will undoubtedly lead to more work down the road.

The example that follows comes from an outstanding account leader I had the pleasure of managing. He was leading a client that was engaged in the deli service sector. He had subscribed to, and read religiously, two key trade publications that related to this client's business. He spotted an article about the challenges in using "all commodity volume" (ACV) product distribution to measure success. Though this had little to do with our work on the business, he forwarded it to the client with the great note included below. This note illustrated his genuine passion and excitement for his client's business. It demonstrated how knowledgeable he was about it. It highlighted his curiosity. And he didn't craft an overly-professional-sounding note that would have been much less interesting. This note comfortably and genuinely expressed his fun and laid-back personality.

Hello.

The good people at Meat & Deli Retailer and Food & Beverage were kind enough to transfer my subscription so I could stay in touch with my roots. Today they sent me a newsletter covering a variety of subjects.

*What really caught my eye was a link to an article, "The Myths and Dangers of ACV." This one hit home and took me back to my days of new product launches where I had to supply ACV goals as a measure of success. Given the Deli Category, it was hard to find good consistent data. Freshlook was always a projection based on a limited number for retailers and regions. We had to use custom aggregates to arrive at our universe for Pre-Sliced in IRI (thereby creating inconsistent ACV-based measures). Yet my team was consistently held to ACV goals. Granted, we could use shipment data to validate, but I always felt that ACV seemed to lack the breadth and depth needed to qualify what was considered a successful product launch. My business relied on both Club Channels and Wal*Mart, neither of which were captured by Freshlook or IRI.*

Naturally, when I saw this article I was curious as to what it might say about those issues. The article lists several myths and things to consider about the use of ACV. Some of these myths I was guilty of subscribing to. I wanted to pass this along to you as some food for thought as you look to future package redesigns and possible new products and/or categories to pursue. The article did not provide an immediate solution, but it may provide good insight if a situation arises where the gut check of a product launch doesn't seem to marry up to the numbers being reported. If nothing else, it is an admission of guilt that I am one of 'those people' who love to talk shop about the deli category!

Thank you for your time.

Partnership impact:

The client called to thank him for the note and proactive thinking. She was genuinely impressed by his knowledge of the category and his interest in her business — and by the fact that the note was not merely a disguised attempt by him to secure more business for his agency. It was simply something he found interesting and relevant — and he assumed his client would, as well. Nothing more. It was a very simple gesture that had a very strong impact.

This account leader was quite new on the business, so this note served a significant role in helping him create a good first impression. As it turns out, the partnership between him and this particular client turned out to be one of the strongest I have seen in my many years in the business.

Lead long-term client planning

Manage your client engagements by taking the initiative in developing, executing and monitoring long-term client plans. This is a great way to signal to your clients your strong leadership skills and passion for growing their businesses.

Practical tips:

- *Develop plans that are client-centric, not agency-centric*. The plans should focus on how you intend to grow *their businesses, not yours.* Remember, if you grow your clients' businesses, your agency's business will grow as a result.

- *Keep these 10 simple principles in mind as you develop and manage client plans:*

    1. *Tell a story*: Don't just provide masses of information. Weave the data and information into a tight story that is clear, concise and compelling.

    2. *Approach it like a journey:* Talk about where you have been, where you want to go and how you intend to get there.

3. *Paint a vision:* Make sure everyone knows what you think is possible and how passionate you are about making it happen. This will generate their excitement, as well.

4. *Compel strong collaboration:* Include cross-functional team members in the planning process. Assign them a role, motivate them and hold them accountable.

5. *Involve your clients:* If you are to succeed in your client planning, your clients need to be aware of — and supportive of — your plans for them.

6. *Continually assess the plan:* Don't treat it like a file document. It needs to be managed and measured. Review progress routinely and implement course corrections when and where deemed appropriate.

7. *Be proactive:* Anticipate potential risks, barriers and challenges — both internal and external — and develop plans to address them.

8. *Be introspective:* Be honest about where you are today in order to truly understand what it will take to arrive where you want to go.

9. *Focus on client value:* Again, the plan should be client-centric. Be clear about — and continually assess — the value it delivers for your clients.

10. *Leverage client value:* Ensure your clients see and appreciate the value they derive from your plans. It is okay to promote the great work you and your agency are doing.

- *Include the following key sections in your client plans:*

    - *Vision:*

        - Articulate a concise, compelling and inspirational statement of what you want to achieve vis-à-vis your client's business.

        - Enumerate key elements that need to be true in order to achieve this vision. This could include items related to the industry, competition, the client's business, etc.

    - *Where you are today:*

        - Provide a summary of the current agency-client relationship, including successes, challenges and opportunities for continual improvement.

        - Identify clearly the client's key business issues and challenges. What keeps the client up at night?

    - *Where you want to go:*

        - Develop a strategic plan. A good tool to consider is an OGSTM — Objectives, Goals, Strategies, Tactics & Measures. Whatever format you employ, make certain it forces you to be clear about what you want to achieve, to make *choices* about how you intend to do so, to clearly identify who needs to do what by when, and to develop clear measures for monitoring progress and course correcting as necessary.

- After you develop a sound strategic plan, identify potential risks, barriers and challenges. Then, to ensure your plan will be delivered as promised, develop methods to overcome these issues.

▪ *Determine the client stakeholders with whom you need to build relationships to help the client win.* If you are managing a large account like Procter & Gamble, trying to build relationships with everyone with whom you come in contact will quickly overwhelm you and your agency team. Instead, focus on the *quality* of relationships, not the *quantity*. And develop a strategic plan for penetrating the client base and building relationships. Identify and prioritize a manageable number of key client stakeholders. This can and should include decision makers, economic purchasers and influencers. They all have an impact. Don't simply pick clients with whom you already have relationships — or with whom you can easily secure meetings. They may not have much or any impact.

Once you have identified key client stakeholders, assign members of your agency team — including your management — ownership responsibilities on a one-to-one basis. At the end of the day you are in a relationship-based business and relationships are best formed on a personal level. You can't manage all the client relationships on your own. Your team members and management are there for a reason. Use them.

Once client relationship owners are identified, lead everyone on your agency team — management included — in the development of concerted plans to establish and build the necessary one-to-one relationships. This should include the following details:

- *Who* are you targeting? Be selective. Be strategic. Make sure you have a manageable number. Remember, a strategy requires sacrifice.

- *Why* are they important? Are they a key decision maker? Do they control the budgets? Do they wield influence in the organization? If so, what kind? With whom?

- *What* is in it for them? Why should they want to build a relationship with you? What do you have to offer? On what need do you and your agency deliver uniquely?

- *When* and *how* should they be contacted? When is the appropriate time to contact them? After the initial contact, how often should you follow-up? In what manner?

Strategically sell in new services

Be a proactive consultant, not a reactionary and near-sighted sales person. Do so by being strategic, client-centric and long-term focused in your selling efforts.

Practical tips:

- *Work with your agency's cross-functional partners (e.g., strategic planners, creatives, analysts, media managers, etc.) to identify client business-building opportunities and develop unsolicited recommendations to attack them.* These recommendations need to marry what the clients need with what your agency offers — and do so in a strategic and sustainable manner. They need to truly create client value. Remember, you are a consultant, not a salesperson.

- *Ensure that every member of your team is participating actively in this proactive process.* While it is your job as the client leader to guide this effort, make certain your team members understand that it is critical to the health of the agency in which they all have a personal financial stake (via bonuses and salary increases at the very least).

- *Pursue opportunities to present these recommendations to the appropriate client contacts and lead their thinking*. If they don't respond, don't give up. Schedule reminders in your calendaring function to follow-up with the clients at reasonable intervals. Don't pester them. But, when you do follow up, ensure them that listening to your ideas will be a good use of their time — because you are focused on building *their* business. You need to turn your great ideas into live projects. You need to create traction and compel action.

- *Don't ever assume that your clients are aware of everything your agency has to offer*. No matter how often you feel you have told them, you can never reinforce it enough. And your agency is likely adding to its tool chest on a regular basis. Be consultative and let your clients know that you simply want to ensure they are getting the maximum value out of their engagements with your agency.

- *Create and share success stories that showcase the breadth and impact of your agency's capabilities*. Real stories are much more impressive than general reviews of capabilities. Note the use of the term "success stories," rather than the standard industry term: "case studies." It is important to stress a focus on generating results. And it is critical to tell a story, not simply share information. There is no universal process for communicating success stories, but I find the following format helpful (it is followed by a real-life example to demonstrate its effectiveness):

    - *Situation:* Provide a brief overview of relevant information. No more than absolutely necessary to set up and justify the actions taken by your agency.

    - *Solution:* Explain the strategies and tactics implemented by your agency to address the problem or leverage the opportunity articulated in the "situation" section.

- *Success:* Showcase the results generated by your agency's work. If possible, secure quantifiable in-market results. At a minimum, find a compelling way to demonstrate your client's satisfaction with the work (e.g., a compelling testimonial). Since your clients generally possess the data and information required to complete this section, you will need to follow up with them after the work is complete, to acquire it. Don't be afraid to be aggressive as you do this. Your clients will assuredly appreciate your interest in the results your agency's work generated for their businesses.

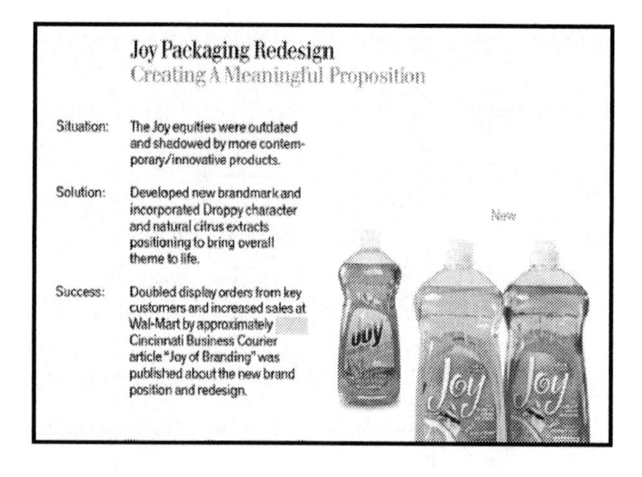

- <u>*Share with your clients the awards your agency wins on their behalf.*</u> Again, don't just *tell* your clients about what you have to offer, *show* how it is making a difference for them and your other clients. Develop promotional materials — like the example that follows — and share with your clients. This effort takes time, but the enhanced impact it will have is certainly worth the incremental effort.

Personal example:
Selling in a new service that adds significant and unprecedented value to a client's business.

One of the more unique clients with which I had the pleasure to work was the chemicals division of a large consumer packaged goods company. This division sells chemical by-products — which are created through the manufacturing of consumer brands — to be used as raw materials by other manufacturers. These chemicals include commoditized items such as glycerin and fatty acid. Not very glamorous, to say the least. But, we were charged with the business-to-business advertising for this division, so we worked diligently to create a compelling and exciting proposition for it.

Due to the generic nature of the products this division sold, this proved to be a very challenging and interesting task. I quickly realized that we needed to change the game a bit if we were going to be successful. In particular, our team needed to start thinking about this division as a brand, rather than a collection of commodities. I approached the global director with a business-building proposition to treat this chemicals division as a brand and, as such, to leverage the branding tools that the company's conventional consumer brands employed. Although my client had virtually no experience in this area, he understood and approved the proposal.

We immediately set out to create a clear and competitively-differentiated brand equity statement, with benefits and reasons-to-believe. We developed a unique brand character, which we brought to life with visuals and words. Once we established the brand's strategic intent, we created a powerful visual identity platform and new executional equity assets, including a new brand mark, selling line and color scheme.

Partnership impact:

This unprecedented branding effort proved to be an overwhelmingly strong success for this client. The global director summarized the results to a colleague in the following note excerpt:

> *[Company] Chemicals has struggled with identity for many years. As you can imagine, being a chemicals operation within a large consumer goods organization presents some unique challenges.*
>
> *Todd Sebastian came to us with a proposition to apply [Company]-type equity and branding principles to [Company] Chemicals. The proposition was attractive and the result has been that for the first time in my almost 30 years with Chemicals we have developed an equity and identity that properly represent our purpose, character and objectives. This is very important in a world of commodities, where margins are razor thin.*
>
> *I am pleased to say that the equity has even carried over to Asia, where our company is a much less well known product. In China, we are now commanding premium prices due to our equity.*

Todd asked me to write to you about our experiences. In my opinion, Todd and his team have been professional and efficient, helping us immensely for reasonable cost. Todd is one of the most knowledgeable people I know on branding and equity.

Personal example:
Creating a win-win business-building bridge for the client and the agency.

Several years ago one of our clients was preparing to launch a new stomach-remedy brand line extension intended for children. As is customary, a few agencies were involved and tasked with specific components of the launch plan. We were given the responsibility for direct-to-consumer and in-store print promotion communications.

During a review of the complete communication plan developed by the multi-agency team, I was surprised by the absence of an influencer marketing component, which would leverage authoritative third parties to build credibility and drive consumer trust. In the case of this brand, I felt there was a significant opportunity to leverage pediatricians and pharmacists to positively influence parents. Historically, these professionals have recommended strictly *against* using the adult version of the brand for children under the age of 12 years old.

Our agency felt a concerted communications effort aimed at these professional targets was necessary. The intent would be to confirm they understood that this line extension is different than the standard brand and is specifically formulated to be safe for children between 2 and 12 years of age. Usually the objective of an influencer marketing program is to encourage an influential third party group to actively recommend a brand/product. In this case, the goal would be to move pediatricians and pharmacists away from negative recommendations to a position of neutrality, at a minimum.

This would ensure that parents would not be steered away from purchasing this line extension by negative professionals who are not fully informed. Ultimately we would encourage these professionals to be positive advocates after they became neutral.

Although influencer marketing was not a core capability of my branding and design agency, it was an area in which I had significant personal experience. I felt my agency's existing skills could be applied with success, so, I was 100% confident we could pull it off for our client's benefit.

Accordingly, I worked with my team to recommend an influencer marketing component for the launch of this line extension. Because our passion for wanting to see the launch succeed came through clearly to the client team, the proposal was accepted. In fact, they were quick to recognize how important it would be to a successful launch, and shifted funding from other components of the plan to award the influencer marketing component the lion's share of their resources.

Partnership impact:

This proved to be a tremendous win-win for the client and for our agency — and the partnership between the two. The client clearly appreciated our proactive and passionate plea to consider influencer marketing. The product launch was a strong success — and the influence generated from pediatricians and pharmacists was cited as a major contributor.

This project helped these clients understand that there was more we could do to help them win — and we were eager to prove our effectiveness. As I mentioned earlier, influencer marketing was not a core capability of my agency. But, it was something I was confident we could offer to expand on our ability to help our clients. We just needed a success story to help us build credibility.

This product launch gave us just that. In fact, it was featured a few months later in a cover story in the *Cincinnati Business Courier*. This article added significant credibility that helped our influencer marketing practice take off — thus allowing us to broaden the help we could offer our clients and giving our agency a significant new revenue stream.

Prepare uniquely for all presentations

Every presentation and meeting is different, depending on what you are covering and with whom. Take the time to prepare for every one in an appropriately tailored fashion, in order to provide the most relevant and persuasive recommendations and consultation.

Practical tips:

- *Re-purpose materials only when it is appropriate.* Senior clients require a different level of content than more junior ones. If you do re-purpose materials, find a simple way to tailor them so your clients don't perceive them as "off the rack" or "generic." You want your clients to feel important. They are.

- *Never show up to a client meeting empty-handed.* Even if your client called the meeting, find out what it is about and bring something that is relevant. This could be a related success story. Or white paper. Or trade publication article. Or a talk sheet with your thoughts. Something. Your preparedness will demonstrate your passion and proactive nature.

- *Always prepare an agenda, even for internal meetings.* Communicate clearly and concisely the meeting purpose, desired outcome(s) and structure (i.e., roles, responsibilities and timing). When possible and appropriate, send the agenda in advance of the meeting. This helps people prepare for the meeting — even if just mentally — and it saves times in the meeting by eliminating the need for an exhaustive upfront review of why everyone is gathered.

- *Be your own most brutal critic as you prepare for all client meetings in which your agency will be presenting work*. Is the work mind-opening? Have you pushed into areas that are uncomfortable (which is a good thing)? Is your vision clearly tied to the strategies and needs of the business? Where are the potential issues? Are you prepared to address these potential issues?

- *Determine your desired client takeaway for all meetings and presentations*. What do you want them to think and say at the end of a meeting? Then, prepare for and conduct the meeting in a manner that will yield this end result.

- *Look for ways to make each presentation fun and interesting*. Do this in a way that is directly relevant and tailored to the purpose of each presentation. Don't entertain simply for entertainment's sake. You have to have a point.

- *Prepare for all presentations in a client-centric manner*. Presentations should not be about your agency, but rather *how your agency can help the client*. Have a clear and powerful point of view (POV) that summarizes your plan to help the client's business.

- *Guide the preparation for presentations with a strategic client brief*. Your agency wouldn't start creative work without a project brief, so why would you begin building an important presentation without one?

Think about the *story* you want to convey. I have been in so many presentation-preparation meetings in which the first question asked is, "What PowerPoint slides do we need?" This is a very ineffective place to initiate action. Until you know what story you intend to tell, how do you know what content and materials are needed? Presentations should be approached in a much more strategic fashion than merely slapping together PowerPoint slides.

To this end, I created a project brief template that I utilize with both current and prospective clients. It covers:

- *Client overview:* Provide a detailed overview of the client's business using a SWOT analysis (strengths, weaknesses, opportunities, threats). Keep this focused and concise (include detailed attachments if necessary).

- *Competition/industry overview:* Create a relevant framework for the presentation by understanding the competitive context. Go beyond what the client furnishes and perform additional research. Conduct store checks and gather samples of competitive brands and products for your team members to experience.

- *Target audience overview:* Provide target audience information. Demographics. Psychographics. Shopping behavior. Consumption habits. Attitudinal perspective. Go beyond what the client furnishes and do supplementary research. Consider creating your own user panel. Set up in-home observations. Whatever it takes to truly understand the target audience.

- *Key client challenges/requests:* Describe in detail what the client indicates they are seeking to accomplish, if not already articulated in a detailed RFP (request for proposal, which should be attached). Capture an understanding of "what keeps the client up at night."

- *Key client need:* This should include articulated and *unarticulated* needs. Ask numerous questions and *listen* to what they say and what they *don't* say. Confirm you and the client agree on their needs.

- *Expected client attendance:* Names. Titles. What do you know about them? What makes them tick? Who are the decision makers? Influencers?

- *Client expectations for presentation/meeting:* Ask your clients what they are specifically expecting to see/hear, so you can meet and exceed their expectations.

- *Pitch competition intelligence (if relevant):* Do you know what other agencies are pitching the business? Are they direct competitors to your agency? If so, review your competitive tracking files (which you should maintain for all key competitors). If not, conduct some research. Learning as much as possible about your competition will help position your agency in the client's mind. What's their equity position? What capabilities, expertise and proprietary tools do they have to support this position? Who is on their client list? What type of work and results do they provide these clients? What awards have they won? What are they saying in press releases and media articles? Who are their leaders and key managers? What do they have to say? "Google" them and find out everything you can.

- *Goal of presentation:* What is the desired outcome — win the business? Secure another meeting? Succeed to the next round of the agency selection process?

- *How your agency is uniquely qualified to exceed the client's needs:* Think about this as your agency's benefit and reasons-to-believe, and do so in relation to your competitors. What are they likely to say? How is your agency different and better? As with any strategic plan, make choices and sacrifices.

- *POV statement:* Once you have determined how you are uniquely qualified to exceed the client's needs, summarize your story in a clear, concise and powerful statement. Ideally, it should be one sentence — written in layman's terms, not consultant-speak. The POV statement should simply sum up the answer to the inevitable client question: "Why should I work with you?"

- *Defining visual:* Once you have nailed your POV statement, bring it to life via a defining visual. This will help the client remember your POV statement, which sums up why they should work with you, thereby articulating the "so what" upfront and creating a compelling context for the forthcoming presentation. You'll see examples of defining visuals at the beginning of each section of this book. In addition, the following example shows how to flow from a defining visual to a POV statement, then to a more detailed explanation of the POV.

This example comes from a presentation to a leading manufacturer of foodservice coffee. Our main POV focused on the company's need to re-configure its unwieldy product line-up. It offered an overwhelming number of product variations — many of which were redundant or didn't fit strategically in the line-up. To convey this POV — and set up why our agency was the best choice to help the client navigate this issue — we developed the following series of slides:

Slide 1:
(This image — in striking color with absolutely no copy to explain it — was projected on the screen as the clients entered the room, in order to create intrigue. Since the image has seemingly nothing to do with foodservice coffee, it really piqued the clients' interest — making them curious as to why it was on the screen.)

Slide 2:

(This slide was projected on the screen after the meeting was underway, in order to explain the intriguing visual and set up our point of view about the client's business.)

Slide 3:

(This slide expanded on our point of view and began to detail our unique qualifications.)

A strong brand requires a clear architecture and compelling identity.

- **We can create a simple and organized brand architecture:**
  - World's leading brand consultancy.
  - 60-year history in creating, managing, and refreshing the world's biggest brands.
- **We can create a holistic and powerful brand identity:**
  - Strong visual and verbal brand identity expertise.

- *Consider carefully the following factors as you begin developing the presentation*:

    - *Assemble the appropriate agency team members.* Identify which members will be in the meeting (with assigned roles and responsibilities) and which will provide behind-the-scenes preparation support.

    - *Think about how you want to kick off the meeting.* Then create a framework within which to tell your unique story.

    - *Develop and agree to a meeting outline and structure.* Don't automatically assume you will use PowerPoint. In fact, you should try to minimize and even eliminate this medium as much as possible. Do something more dynamic, interesting and unexpected.

      In the following example from a design kick-off meeting, we captured the project objective, challenges and strategies, on presentation boards that we mounted in the window frames of the conference room.

      Since the project pertained to a new fruit-scented product, we accompanied these communication boards with inspirational and beautiful images of fruit — and supported these images with elegant props on the conference table.

      A picture of the conference room follows, to showcase how these unique presentation elements came together to create a dynamic and exciting — and unexpected — atmosphere:

- *Develop a team task list that clearly articulates who is responsible for what.* Clearly identify the content and who is responsible for creating it and presenting it.

- *Look for opportunities to provide insights, observations, considerations, or recommendations — whatever is most relevant for the situation.* Remember, you must focus on how you can uniquely help the client. And you need to demonstrate initiative, strategic thought leadership, and the ability to consult with confidence. Be careful not to stretch your proactive consultation beyond your knowledge base, though. You don't want to present clients the opportunity to poke holes in ideas that are off-base for reasons that you were not aware of — therefore causing your good intentions to go awry.

- *Prepare the room and choreograph the presentation.* Develop a plan for how to utilize the space in the room in which the presentation is to take place. If in a client's conference room, try to survey it in advance, if at all possible. Plan every detail. Where will the A/V equipment be placed? Presentation boards? Where do you want the clients to be positioned? Where will your team be? Do you want to exploit different parts of the room to deliver different parts of the presentation? If so, how will it flow? The more you familiarize yourself with the space and how you plan to use it, the more prepared and confident you will be.

Personal example:
Approaching a standard presentation in a non-standard, client-centric manner.

Our team needed to welcome and orient a design manager who was new to one of our client companies and its beauty care business that we managed. Since he was positioned to ultimately be based in the UK, and we were stationed in the Cincinnati office of our global branding and design agency, we would not be working directly with this new client on a day-to-day basis.

As we developed a plan of attack for our meeting, we took this situation into account. Accordingly, we chose to position our Cincinnati office as a great *resource* for this new client. This positioning had several relevant components: we were a global resource, a North America resource, a beauty care resource, a resource for general knowledge of his company, and a resource for understanding the specific company design tools he needed to learn. We detailed this plan of attack in a thorough presentation brief, using the format shared previously in this chapter.

Once we agreed on this direction, we crafted a clear and concise point of view statement. It simply proclaimed, “We have the tools to be a great beauty care resource to you in your new role." We brought this POV statement to life with the following defining visual:

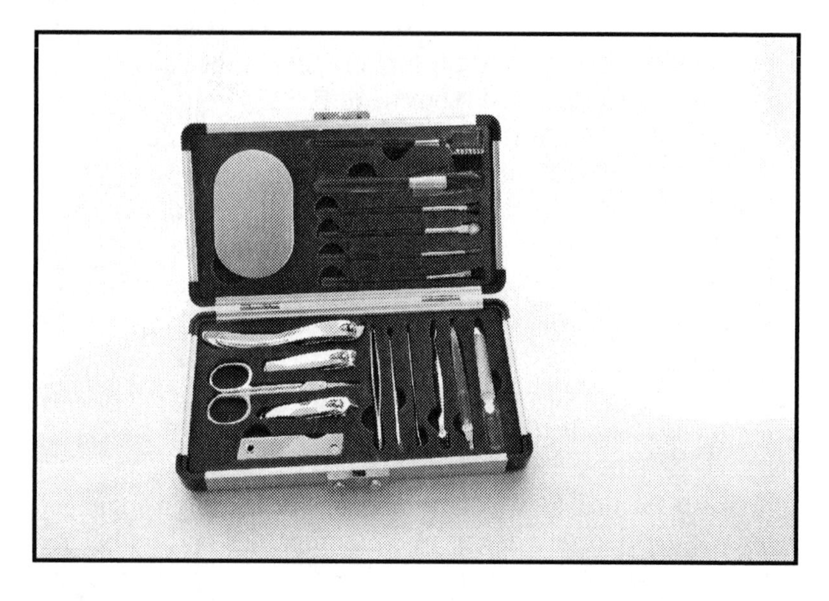

This elegant visual was projected on a large screen as the client entered the conference room. It was significantly more interesting than seeing a standard opening slide stating something expected, such as "Agency Orientation" with the client's name and the date. Shortly into the meeting we revealed the POV statement, which explained the purpose of this visual and our desired intent for the forthcoming meeting.

In addition to this motivating POV statement and defining visual, we developed an appropriate and engaging approach to the presentation. Rather than using PowerPoint (which is expected, dull and quickly tiring), we created a "design fair." In our planning meeting we identified several success stories we wanted to share. We then created several "stations" in the conference room in which each individual success story could be told. There was no conference table or chairs. At each station the key phases of each project were demonstrated through some physical material (e.g., sketches, boards, mock-ups, presentation decks, etc.). The team literally walked the client from station to station, rather than planting him in a chair and presenting to him for two hours. A very refreshing approach. And it created a perfect forum within which to demonstrate knowledge of his company, our capabilities, and our success stories — all of which are resources for him to leverage. So, we executed our strategic intent for the meeting perfectly.

Beyond this appropriate approach to the meeting, we also spent time preparing details that are often overlooked. For instance, rather than bringing in the standard fare of refreshments, we went out of our way to find traditional English items that would help him feel at home. A nice touch — and one that was clearly appreciated by the client.

Partnership impact:

This unique approach to the meeting was evident to the client as soon as he walked in the room, exclaiming, "Wow … this isn't going to be a standard agency orientation!" Given the power of first impressions, we definitely achieved a great start with this new client. We could have taken the easy route and simply presented our "off the rack" capabilities presentation. And in doing so, we would have met his expectations. Instead, what we did admittedly required a lot more effort, but the client's recognition and appreciation made the extra effort 100% worthwhile.

Always send meeting summaries

Every client project is a journey. And you're leading it. In order to make sure you are on course to deliver a project with success, you need to know if your team is on track at all times. You must also be on the same page with your client at all times.

A highly-effective way to accomplish this is to document all key agreements and indicated actions in meeting summaries. They are tedious and time consuming, but will undoubtedly save you more time than they take. And the project documentation will definitely prevent headaches if you and your agency discover you're on a different track than your clients.

Practical tips:

- *Close all client meetings by clearly, accurately and concisely summarizing all key discussion points and next steps*. Do this even if the key points are obvious and everyone seems to be in full agreement. It never hurts to be on the safe side.

- *Follow up all client meetings with a written meeting summary*. It is critical to capture agreements in writing. This initiative will demonstrate how buttoned up you are — which will reinforce that you can be counted on — and it will help avoid any misunderstandings between your agency and your clients (and your agency will always be on the short end if details are not documented).

- *For particularly important and/or complex meetings, follow up with a formal document that covers:*

    - *Meeting objective:* A very concise overview of the purpose of the meeting.

    - *Meeting overview:* A concise and general headline indicating how the meeting went — stated as objectively as possible. For example: "The client team indicated that it was pleased with the concepts presented by the agency."

    - *Key discussion points and agreements:* This is not intended to be a recap of the entire meeting, but rather a summary of the most relevant points. I suggest you capture each item in a simple bullet-point format for easy review.

    - *Key next steps:* Make certain to capture everything in a "who/what/when" format. It is critical to assign single-point ownership and clear delivery dates to all action items, so nothing falls through the cracks.

- *Create a note-taking template to use in meetings.* Writing meeting summaries can be an arduous and time-consuming process. But, it is very important. Using a note-taking template will make the process much more efficient and effective. If your note-taking template matches the format of your meeting summaries, you won't have to weed through your notes looking for the appropriate content — and potentially miss something important. To that end, consider creating a document similar to the example that follows. Run a stack of copies and keep them in a handy place to take to meetings.

<table>
<tr><th colspan="3">Meeting Notes Template</th></tr>
<tr><td colspan="3">Attendees:
▪ Client:
▪ Agency:

Date:</td></tr>
<tr><td colspan="3">Meeting objective:</td></tr>
<tr><td colspan="3">Meeting overview:</td></tr>
<tr><td colspan="3">Discussion / agreements:
▪
▪
▪</td></tr>
<tr><td colspan="3">Next steps:</td></tr>
<tr><td>Who</td><td>What</td><td>When</td></tr>
<tr><td>▪
▪
▪</td><td>▪
▪
▪</td><td>▪
▪
▪</td></tr>
</table>

- *For meetings that don't require a formal summary, utilize a simple and informal e-mail to capture the key points and next steps.* The point is to create some form of a summary every time you and your clients agree to something. Even if you have a brief phone conversation in which you agree to something simple, follow-up the call with a quick e-mail. If all that is required is one short sentence, so be it. Keep in mind that clients do, in fact, want to see some semblance of a summary. I have often received client complaints when summaries are not provided. One client suggested, "They don't have to be fancy. Just a simple e-mail sometimes is enough. The key is to do them in a consistent and timely manner."

- *Regardless of the type of summary you create and send, always include attachments of any work that is referenced.* Don't expect your clients to have the work committed to memory. For example, if you write a summary for a meeting in which several print ads were presented, attach copies of each ad. Since most documents are sent via e-mail nowadays, attach the ads in PDF form. And rather than expect your client to work by opening up several e-mail attachments, be considerate and string them together into one PDF. Or, better yet, embed the electronic images directly into the document, so your clients can quickly and easily cross-reference the work with the comments and articulated next steps. It doesn't take much time to expend these extra efforts and clients will appreciate them.

- *Take the opportunity to show passion and excitement for the project and thank the clients for their time.* These are nice gestures that show you care. This can be done in the beginning of the actual meeting summary or, if you are sending the summary in the form of an e-mail attachment, you can cover this in the body of the e-mail.

- *When sending meeting summaries via e-mail as document attachments, don't just say, "See attached" – or worse, send a blank e-mail.* Take the opportunity in the body of the e-mail message to thank your clients again for their time, and to summarize the key points of the attached summary. Yes, this is basically summarizing the summary. But a little more work by you reduces the amount of work for your clients.

- *Distribute a summary within 24 hours of meetings.* Given how quickly things move in today's world, meeting summaries need to be timely in order to be relevant.

- *Use a meeting summary as a tool to kick off the follow-up meeting, so everyone is reminded of key discussion points and agreements in the last meeting.* Review "next steps" in detail to ensure nothing fell through the cracks. Clarify that everyone agrees on the current status before you proceed with the meeting. There is no sense pushing forward if you are not all on the same track.

Personal example:
Summarizing a meeting in a timely manner.

Within two hours of a very important client meeting one outstanding member of my account team distributed a very thorough meeting summary. It leveraged all the tips outlined in this section, including the suggestion of embedding in the document the key images of the work that was presented, to create a helpful context for the comments in the meeting summary.

Partnership impact:

It takes time and effort to create a sound meeting summary. But, it is critically important. Moreover, and contrary to conventional wisdom, clients do appreciate good meeting summaries. In this case, the key client responded to the meeting summary with the following note, "Thank you for your speedy response and thorough recap. Your reference document is a great communication tool and can help us stay aligned and on track for this project and future work. You have set a new standard for us! Thanks again."

Communicate, communicate, communicate

Most client-related issues can be avoided — or at least solved expeditiously — with clear, open and timely communication. Establish this as a hallmark of how you lead all of your client relationships.

Practical tips:

- *If you sense an issue is developing, deal with it proactively, aggressively and positively.* Don't hide from it. The quicker you deal with it, the less severe it will become and the quicker it will go away. And the less negative potential impact it will have on your partnership. Even if you are not responsible for creating the issue, take accountability for it on behalf of your agency. Act like the positive leader you need to be, engage your clients openly and honestly, and work together to resolve it. Clients will appreciate your leadership and accountability — thus turning potential negatives into positive impacts on your partnerships.

- *Don't discuss issues with clients via e-mail.* Ever. This is a terribly ineffective medium for potentially contentious dialogue. Have an in-person conversation. If this is not feasible, at a minimum, implement a live telephone conversation. Keep the tone positive.

Allow for a give-and-take exchange. Allow your clients to be heard. Allow your clients to fully understand your position. E-mail does not allow for this.

- *Pay close attention to content and text, in all forms of written and oral communication*. As the face of your agency, it is critical that you communicate effectively. You represent your agency by what you say and how you say it. If your e-mails are full of typos, what does that say about the professionalism of your agency and the quality of work your clients can expect?

- *To avoid embarrassing or damaging gaffes, employ spell-check religiously*. In fact, set it to run automatically in your word processing and e-mail programs. However, given that "your" and "you're" may be spelled correctly, but used improperly, make one final effort for accuracy before sending, by reading your e-mail aloud. If your PDA does not have a spell-check option, set your automatic signature to read something to the effect of, "Sent from my wireless handheld. Please excuse any typos." Creating mistake-free messages is more difficult on a "two-thumb" PDA keyboard, but at least your clients will know that you strive for accuracy and care when it is not achieved.

Spend time strategically

Being a client leader is a very demanding job. How you spend your time has a profound impact on your level of success. Therefore, you need to treat time as your most precious resource. There is no limit to the things on which you *could* spend your time. You must make strategic choices on how and where you *will* spend it.

Practical tips:

- *Since the most important aspect of your job is to build client partnerships, the very first choice you should make is to devote as much of your time as possible to being with your clients.* You can't build relationships if you are physically absent from them. One of my all-time favorite quotes comes from John le Carré, an English suspense novelist who proclaimed, "A desk is a dangerous place from which to watch the world." Well, it is also a dangerous place from which to try and build client partnerships. This may seem like an obvious point. But, it is often forgotten as our schedules become increasingly hectic and overwhelming.

- *When you are not physically with clients, you should try to focus as much of your time as possible on activities which benefit them.* You should be thinking constantly about your clients' businesses, whether you are with them or not.

- *If forced to make a choice, choose to spend time with current clients over prospective new clients.* Some agency veterans may disagree with this point of view. But, if you truly believe in the power of client partnerships, you will always choose to properly maintain and build current relationships before trying to foster new ones. I firmly believe that the best source of new business is current clients. It is much more efficient and effective to leverage the credibility you worked so hard to establish with current clients, than it is to start from scratch with prospective new clients.

  And keep in mind that loyalty is a two-way proposition. You can't expect your current clients to remain loyal to you if you are constantly absent trying to woo new clients. Plus, if you thoroughly satisfy your current clients, they will serve as your most powerful new business drivers via word-of-mouth referrals and positive endorsements.

- *Spend as little time as possible on internal administrative activities that yield no client benefits.* There are things you simply must do (e.g., timesheets). Just try to be as efficient as possible, so you can free up more time for client-centric work.

- *Consider identifying all the internal and external things that could occupy your time. Then develop a plan for how you should strive to allocate your time.* List all key activities and the percentage of your time you hope to devote to them. Track your plan for a week or two and see if you are, in fact, spending time where you had intended. You will likely be surprised by how easily and significantly you fell off track, given the relentless demands on your time. As a starting point, here are some activities to take into consideration:

- *Client presentations:* Presenting new strategy and/or creative work to current clients. No matter how junior you are, push your management for as many opportunities as possible to be actively involved in presentations. In this business you can never practice presenting enough or become too polished at it. Even if you don't have a formal role in the presentation, learn from watching your superiors.

- *Client meetings:* Meetings with current clients in which you are not presenting work. Look for opportunities to meet face-to-face with your clients as much as possible. And be active in every meeting you attend, regardless of your level and how many layers of your management are in the room. Clients become quickly frustrated with agency people who don't talk and add value in meetings, because they know they are paying for their time, to be there.

- *Proactive proposals:* All work related to thinking about, developing, and selling-in unsolicited business-building ideas to current clients. The more senior your role, the more time you should be spending in this area — and the more results you should be generating with your proposals, for your clients.

- *New business:* All work related to preparing for and securing new business with new clients. New business is a fun and rewarding experience for everyone in the agency world.

Attain some as soon as possible and try to stay involved throughout your career. But, always make your current client partnerships a higher priority.

- *Internal meetings:* Meetings in which clients are not involved, but client work is being discussed. The more senior you are, the less time you should spend in these types of meetings. Rely on your more junior team members. You need to become increasingly comfortable delegating responsibilities in order to ease the burden on your schedule and, at the same time, allow your subordinates an opportunity to learn and grow, by actually doing the work.

- *Administration:* Internal activities not directly related to client work, including timesheets, billing, estimates, meeting summaries, etc. Most agencies have escalating hourly billing rates — and for good reason. The more senior you are, the more valuable is your time. Spend as much time as possible building client partnerships, not performing administrative work.

Optimize the positive impact of proposals

Never underestimate the impact proposals and budget estimates can have on your current and prospective client partnerships. They should not be treated simply as administrative "necessary evils." When managed strategically and properly, they can have a positive impact on your partnerships. When managed poorly, they can have a devastating effect.

Practical tips:

- *NEVER surprise your clients with budget estimates.* Instead, have a verbal discussion with your clients regarding scope and budget expectations on new projects. Let them know what you're thinking and see what they think. If you don't pin down your verbal agreement to a specific number, which you may not be able to do without first meeting with your team and/or management and getting more information, at least try to agree to a range. This verbal discussion and agreement will ensure that your clients are not surprised by the written estimate that will follow.

- *Once you have reached a verbal agreement with your client on at least general expectations around project scope and budget, follow up with a written estimate within 1-3 business days (unless you agree up front to different timing)*. This demonstrates your passion for the work and your commitment to initiate it.

- *If the full extent of the project scope is not known at the time of the project kick-off, develop a phased proposal and only estimate the phases that are manageable at the present time*. This demonstrates your flexibility and willingness to do as much as you can to move the client's work forward.

- *NEVER surprise your clients with budget overages or billing issues*. Instead, take the initiative to keep your clients abreast of your agency's time accrual or billing progress, relative to budget estimates. To this end, request billing updates from your finance department so you can monitor progress. If you do this consistently, you will be able to anticipate potential issues well before they become actual issues.

  If you do, in fact, identify potential concerns, probe deeper to diagnose them and develop plans to rectify them. Then, engage your clients. Share with them the potential issues and the steps you already developed to address them. Your clients probably won't like the fact that there are potential issues, but they will certainly appreciate your proactive, upfront, honest and diligent approach to managing them.

- *If your proposal is for an unsolicited idea that you intend to share proactively with a client, GREAT! ... But be strategic in how you go about selling it*. Think carefully about this on a case-by-case basis. Just sending it via e-mail — although simple — is almost always *not* the best way to present it. Consultants don't try to sell things via e-mail; they make personal sales calls. It is much more effective to consult and build relationships in person. E-mail is extremely impersonal. In addition, it doesn't allow for dialogue. If you can't meet in person, at least have a live telephone conversation. Let your clients see, or at least hear, your passion for your ideas. Offer them a chance to ask questions and seek clarification. The more they understand the ideas, the more likely they are to buy them. Once they understand them, approve them, and agree to a general budget range, *then* send them a written proposal via e-mail.

- *Spur your clients to action through well-written proposals.* The better your written recommendations are the better your clients will understand them, be motivated by them and accept them. A good written recommendation generally includes the following:

    - *A strong opening:* The first paragraph should include an overview of all the details necessary to make the decision. It generally begins with, "This recommends …" followed by a headline of the proposed strategic idea, the objective, budget estimate, and proposed timing. Don't be overly business-like (i.e., dull!) in this section, though. Express your genuine passion and excite your clients, as well. Lastly, whether or not the recommendations are solicited by your clients, take the time to *thank* them for the opportunity to provide the recommendations. This is such a simple gesture. But, it is so powerful, because virtually no one does it. I have had so many clients comment on this gesture, because they have never had an agency thank them before, for the opportunity to bid on work — especially from an agency that already works on the account (and, thus, tends to take it for granted).

    - *Background:* This section includes contextual information and data that are necessary for the recipient to approve the recommendation. Nothing more. Don't underestimate this section. It provides the set up for the sale.

- *Recommendation:* Restate your recommendation in detail. But, be clear and concise. List any and all project elements and/or phases that bring the recommendation to life.

- *Rationale:* This section is critically important. You must communicate persuasively to your clients why they should care. Beyond a passionate subjective argument, leverage objective data and facts where appropriate. Providing this objective perspective makes it much more difficult for clients to argue with your recommendations, and thus makes the selling process much easier. Refer to any data, charts or exhibits that you attach to the recommendation.

- *Implementation:* Provide a detailed explanation of how your recommended idea will be implemented, including a detailed — but not overwhelming — timeline. If it is too detailed, attach it, refer to it, and summarize it in this section.

- *Next steps:* First and foremost, overtly ask for the sale. Don't be shy. You won't secure it if you don't ask for it. Then, set a timeframe and a plan to seek the client's response. Indicate if and when you plan to follow up, or if you would like the client to respond at their convenience. Generally speaking I recommend the former over the latter. It takes the burden off your client and ensures that a follow-up discussion will happen.

Personal example:
Leveraging objective perspective to simplify the sale.

We were involved in a highly-competitive pitch to become the branding and design agency of record for a new-to-the-world pharmaceutical brand. Brand new brands are by far the most fun on which to work, because there are no pre-determined notions regarding the brand's strategic and executional equities. You're awarded a rare chance to work on a truly blank canvas. However, this also makes the work extremely difficult — particularly as you try to convince the client that your ideas are right for the brand.

We felt that the best way to sell our strategic thinking and imaginative work was to move beyond subjective persuasion, by substantiating our position with objective data and perspective. While it's nice to think that great work always speaks for itself, it doesn't. So, we set out to educate the prospective clients on proven design theory and leverage the principles to our advantage. Colors, shapes, patterns, typography and textures all have a specific and proven psychological impact on people. We used our knowledge and expertise on these effects as objective support for our design recommendations. Every single design choice we made was supported by objective rationale. For example:

- *Nave blue* = credible and dependable (perfect for a serious pharmaceutical drug like this one).

- *Bright blue* = vibrant (which is how we wanted the intended female target group to feel).

- *Golden yellow* = comforting and warm (to ease the target's concerns about the drug).

- *Concentric arcs* = hopeful feeling of endless possibilities (which ties directly back to the communication strategy we recommended).

Partnership impact:

The client loved the detail with which we presented our strategic and executional brand equity choices. Ultimately, we won the business. During the meeting in which the client awarded it to us, they pointed to our objective rationale as the key to our victory. They claimed it made us stand out from our competitors, all of whom simply tried to convince the client that their opinions were right, based on their personal expertise.

Maintain good manners

Good manners are important in any interpersonal relationship. A client relationship is no exception. Displaying good manners is just as important in your business life as it is in your personal life. Good manners show you are a good person. Being a good person garners trust and respect. Trust and respect help build partnerships.

Practical tips:

- *When meeting with your clients, turn your mobile phone or PDA to quiet or vibrate.* Grant your clients your undivided attention. Even if your clients know you have other clients, there is no need to rub that fact in their faces. When you are meeting with a particular client, be there for *that* client only.

- *Deliver on promises.* Don't make your clients follow up with you on your promises. If they ultimately have to follow through on your tasks, they will quickly lose confidence in you. Never let them beat you to the punch.

- *Say "Thank you."* Often. It's a simple two-word statement, but it can have a profoundly-positive impact. Thank your clients for their time after meetings or telephone calls. Thank them for the opportunity to work with them. To build their precious brands with them. For their trust in you and your agency. For the opportunity to secure more work. As noted previously, build a genuine statement of appreciation into the opening paragraph of every project proposal. Keep a stock of "Thank You" cards in your desk so you can send personalized, hand-written notes to your clients. While you're at it, maintain a stock of cards for other occasions, as well (e.g., birthdays, baby births, anniversaries, etc.).

- *Say "Hi" at the beginning of e-mails and "Have a good day" at the end.* When seeing your clients in person, you don't just walk up to them and start talking about a certain topic, do you? No, you greet them with a smile, a handshake and a friendly salutation. When the meeting is over, you end with some semblance of a warm gesture. *Why would you not do the same in an e-mail?* E-mail communication is already overly impersonal. But it is, by far, the most commonly used communication medium. So don't be lazy. Take a few extra seconds and display some good manners. Your e-mails will stand out from the hundreds of other messages your clients receive every day, and you will be appreciated and remembered for it.

- *Say "I'm sorry."* Admitting fault and mistakes shows you are *accountable*. It shows you're human and a good human being. It shows you care. It shows you are a partner on which your clients can count. Some people think admitting fault and mistakes makes them look unreliable. Not true. It's just the opposite. If your clients discover your mistakes before you tell them, *then* they will question your dependability and honesty. But, if you admit your errors in a proactive and honest fashion, your clients will never feel the temptation to question you in the future. They will know they can count on you. They will know you are a good person. They will know you are a great partner.

- *After you resolve a conflict, take the time to document the resolution.* This will demonstrate to your client your sincerity in rectifying errors and avoiding recurrences. Create a resolution document template for this purpose. In the heading of this template state something to the effect of, "This serves as official documentation that a specific project issue has been addressed with our team and resolved via a solution and/or process change in order to ensure there are no recurrences." This template should clearly capture the issue and the solution (including any systemic process improvements that have been implemented).

Personal example:
Showing sensitivity to a client's concern.

One of my account teams presented the results of a competitive audit to a group of clients and received an underwhelming response. The clients felt the learning was a little light and, as a result, questioned the value of the audit. The account team did a good job of justifying the audit and the clients ended the meeting by saying they felt better about the situation.

Given the positive ending of the meeting, my account team could have justifiably felt that everything was okay and no further action was required. But, the leader of this team — an experienced vice president — didn't feel right about things. His instinctive feelings led him to investigate the situation further and send the clients the following note:

> *Hi team. Some of the comments made on yesterday's conference call have been weighing heavily on me. The last thing I want to hear as the person responsible for*

serving your business is that you are not seeing value in our work. As a result, I went back and reviewed the proposal which outlined both the process and deliverable for the Competitive Landscape Audit. And to be honest, I understand why you are feeling a bit under-whelmed.

The purpose of conducting a Competitive Landscape Audit is to provide an understanding of the brand positions currently being "claimed" by the brands in a given competitive set. This, in turn, allows us to create and validate unique positions that connect with consumers and differentiate from competitors. The primary method for determining these positions is to pore over and analyze any and all brand communications, be it an annual report, TV and radio copy, FSIs, DTCs, websites, etc. But as we have all come to realize, there is not a whole lot of brand communications happening in this category ... thus not a lot of materials to analyze.

Ultimately, this is a fantastic opportunity for us to carve out a relevant position and make some noise in this uniquely quiet category. However, the report that explains why we believe we can do this is unfortunately fairly thin. Please be assured that we have done our due diligence in trying to uncover these competitive communications. But, in the end, we did not find the amount we expected or for which we budgeted. Given this, it doesn't seem appropriate to charge you for the full estimated amount of this phase of the project. We will bill you only for the actual amount of time accumulated on this phase of the project. With the remaining money in the budget I would like to propose one of the following strategies:

1. *Take the money and run — We will simply reduce the agreed upon amount of the project.*

2. *Pass it down — We can apply the leftover budget to another part of the project ... perhaps add to the quantitative research recruitment.*

3. *Vegas!*

In all seriousness, I want you to know that we place a tremendous value on our partnership. Our sincere hope is that you would come to us if you have any questions about our process or deliverables. We aim to make ourselves so knowledgeable and indispensable to your business that you would want to involve us in all branding and design projects. And this only happens when you feel that are receiving value from our efforts. Please call me if you have any questions. I would be happy to discuss this further.

Thank you!

Your partner.

Partnership impact:

This account person acted with accountability and clearly turned a potential negative into a positive. He could have done nothing, since the clients indicated at the end of the meeting that they were feeling better. Or, sensing that the clients may still have some concerns (though not articulated), the account person could have followed up with an attempt to simply further justify the agency's work. Or, worse, he could have become defensive. He might have felt justified in doing so — since the agency completed the work it was contracted to do — but this would have inevitably led to a negative result.

Instead, he showed that he is good person and a great partner. He demonstrated passion, accountability, sincerity, transparency — and even a little humor to bring some levity to the situation. Basically, he showed good manners. And in a proactive fashion. As a result, the agency-client relationship was strengthened, not weakened.

Inspire internal team

In order to generate the best work possible for your clients, you need to motivate every member of your internal team to be and bestow their best. Don't simply manage your internal team members; motivate and inspire them.

Practical tips:

- *Invite all cross-functional team members to project kick-off meetings.* Keep everyone in the loop and share with them a sense of ownership at the very earliest stages of every project, even if some of the team members won't touch the project for months, due to their back-end roles.

- *Afford your team reasonable project timelines with which to work.* To this end tactfully push back on clients demanding unreasonable timing. Your team and your agency need to be set up for success, not failure. Ultimately, this is in your clients' best interests. Ensure they understand. Your diplomatic assertiveness will establish you as a better partner and demonstrate your strong leadership skills.

- *Impart your team with clear and thorough direction and information up front in the process.* But, don't data dump. Distill the project orientation down to a digestible degree. *Make sure the brief is actually brief!* This is one key way in which you can and should add value, internally. If project briefs from your clients are unclear, work with the clients to make the briefs better before sharing them with your internal team. This is another great way to add value to the process.

- *Consider sending the brief to particularly important internal team members in advance of the project kick-off meeting.* This could include your key strategic planning and/or creative counterparts. This will allot them time to think through the brief and come to the meeting prepared and ready to contribute.

- *Make sure the project brief is in every internal touch-base meeting and review it in advance of the work.* Even if your team is reviewing the tenth iteration of the work, you still need to ensure everyone is re-grounded in the strategy, so everyone is on the same page and commenting on the work objectively.

- *Clearly recap key discussion points at the end of every internal review meeting.* Then, follow up with a summary e-mail to the team, so nothing falls through the cracks. This is a little extra work on your part, but it will be seen as valuable and helpful by the members of your internal team. They count on you for clear and consistent project leadership. The more you provide, the more they will appreciate the value you are adding to their work.

- *In addition to the standard project brief, think about other materials that might inspire the team to do their best work.* This could include marketing materials (e.g., print ads, brochures, etc.), client product, competitive product, and other "show & tell" items. And think about ways to make the meeting fun. You are not just sharing information; you are leading an important process. Don't just make copies of the project brief five minutes before the kick-off meeting, show up, and read the brief to everyone. That is not adding value. Your job is to lead. To energize and excite your team. And ultimately, to make sure the work your team delivers to your clients is as strong as possible.

- *Grant every member of your internal team some direct access to your clients in both professional and social settings.* You don't always have to be a two-way communication filter. Let your team hear directly from your clients and provide them a chance to build direct professional and personal relationships. The more your team members understand and appreciate your clients, the more educated and inspired they will be to deliver truly outstanding work for your clients.

- *Don't just lead your internal team members, roll up your sleeves and help them.* If they are staying late to prepare for a client presentation, offer to stay with them and help in any way you can. Even if you have no creative skills whatsoever, there are things you can do. Help bind the presentation booklets. Cut presentation boards. Offer moral support. Buy pizza. Show you care.

I received the following note in reference to one of my account team members from one of our designers: "Well everything finally came together for the presentation and I wanted to give a special thank you to Anita and Marshal for staying all the way to the wee hours of the morning to see and help make the presentation a success. It's not everyday you see leadership and account executives helping us designers every step of the way, so I just wanted to say thank you for the team effort. Beth and I appreciate your cheering, cutting, and most of all Marshall….your binding skill ☺." As the leader of an account team, I love getting these kinds of notes.

- *Furnish your internal team members a summary of client feedback after every presentation in which they are not present.* Don't wait until the next internal meeting to do this. Send out a quick e-mail or, even better, find your team members and tell them in person. They put plenty of passion into their work and are anxious to learn how it was received by your clients. Don't expect them to wait. And take advantage of this opportunity to thank your team members again for their hard work. You cannot thank them enough.

- *If changes have been requested by a client, do not e-mail them to your internal team members.* That is the easiest method of sharing, but the least effective. Instead, hand deliver the changes to avoid wasting time. More often than not changes need to be turned around quickly. So, every hour counts. If an e-mail sits unread in your team members' inboxes, this will cut into the time they have to work on the changes. A live conversation will not only save time, it will also allow your team members to ask questions on the spot, and make sure they fully understand the client's request. It is your job to certify the feedback loop is closed. To this end, live conversations are your best tool.

Personal example:
Inspiring a team with a creative approach to a project kick-off.

Our agency was about to kick off a major brand redesign project for a pasta sauce brand. At the time, the brand stood for "Inspired Italian." So the account leader in my group applied the coaching in this chapter and set out to create an inspiring project kick-off that would get the team excited and the project off to great start. A few days before the internal team kick-off meeting, she left the following note — beautifully printed on elegant paper — on everyone's chair.

> *Inspire yourself tonight!*
>
> *In preparation for the [Brand] Redesign kick-off meeting on Monday, we are asking each of you to experience the brand for yourself. The task is simple ... and the payoff should be quite enjoyable. A slow-simmered, hand-crafted, Italian-inspired meal in the comfort of your own home. Does it get any better than this?!?*
>
> *Your assignment is to go to the store and select a pasta sauce flavor to buy. Please note the following as you are shopping:*
>
> 1) *Did you have a particular flavor in mind that you wanted to buy before you approached the shelf?*
> 2) *If so, were you able to easily find it?*
> 3) *If not, how did you select a flavor?*
> 4) *What compelled you to choose this flavor?*
> 5) *How long did it take you to find/select what to buy?*
> 6) *What did you find frustrating? Helpful?*
> 7) *Did you find your flavor through verbal or visual cues?*
>
> *Take your pasta sauce home and use it in a meal sometime before Monday. Keep a pad of paper by*

you as you prepare the meal and take notes on the experience. We're looking for your complete experience including sights, sounds, and smells. What did you find particularly memorable or unique as you opened the jar? Poured the sauce? Cooked it? Served it? Tasted it? Were there particular textures, colors, or even images that were evoked through your experience?

Jot down your thoughts and come prepared to share!

Of note, in addition to this great letter, she also provided everyone with coupons to purchase two products for free. Nice touch.

Partnership impact:

This fantastic project kick-off idea had a profoundly positive effect on the client partnership. First and foremost, the client really appreciated the extraordinary effort of the account leader (she kept the client in the loop on her plans for the internal kick-off meeting). She demonstrated tremendous passion for the brand, inspirational leadership, and a desire to make the work better. Secondly, it definitely made the work better. Creatives do their best work when they fully understand what they are working on and they are inspired.

The homework assignment in advance of the project kick-off meeting also forced everyone on the internal team to go to a grocery store, shop the category, take the product home, and try it. To experience everything a shopper and a consumer would experience. To become much more familiar with the brand on which they would be working. To develop a true affinity for it. How could this *not* lead to better work?

Manage your management

When managed properly by you, your management can help develop stronger client partnerships. Demonstrate your leadership by showing them how they can help you.

Practical tips:

- *Look for ways to insert your management into the process of building your client partnerships.* Take the lead on determining where they can have the most impact and tell them how they can help. Don't make your management do the work in figuring this out. If there is a high-level manager on the client side with whom you think your manager should engage, say so. And develop a plan for them. I guarantee they will appreciate your leadership behavior.

- *Keep your management in the loop in a proactive and focused manner.* Leave them quick messages soon after key client meetings in which important developments take place. Just provide necessary top-line updates (i.e., indicate whether it was a good or bad meeting and why). Don't be afraid to share bad news as well as good. Consistently unbalanced sharing of news will cause suspicion. Not everything can go smoothly.

- *If issues arise, let your management know immediately*. They can't help you solve the issues if they are not made aware of them in a timely fashion.

- *If you go to your management with issues, also bring recommended solutions for solving them*. Don't simply dump problems on their laps and expect them to do all the heavy lifting in developing solutions.

Personal example:
Leveraging upper management to build stronger client partnerships.

In a previous chapter focused on maintaining contact with key clients you discovered the idea of creating a "Client in Residence" program. The primary goal of this 13-week client hosting plan was to improve my client's understanding of our agency and our approach to work. But it also afforded my client a wonderful opportunity to become more familiar with everyone on her team at the agency — and for our team to know her.

To this end, I took advantage of my client's presence in our office once a week for 13 weeks, and scheduled one-to-one lunches with her and key people at the agency. This included my CEO. The two had met before and spent some time together, but never one on one.

Partnership impact:

As with personal relationships, professional working relationships are built on trust, respect and communication. This simple one-to-one lunch between my client and my CEO went a long way in establishing all three.

Though the concept of lunch meetings is hardly breakthrough, client leaders rarely make the effort to orchestrate them between their management and key clients. I believe this is the case for a few reasons. First, most client leaders aren't certain if their management considers this a good use of their time — especially the CEO. Therefore, they don't want to waste their management's time and/or they are hesitant to ask. Secondly, due to the controlling nature of client leaders — which, generally speaking, is a good trait for them to exhibit — they are nervous about their clients meeting with their management. Since the client leaders would not be in the meetings, they are concerned about the feedback their clients might provide and promises their management might make.

On the first point, I would encourage you to never question whether or not it is a good use of your management's time to meet with your clients. Your agency's success depends on productive working relationships with clients. Therefore, client engagement is everyone's responsibility — from the CEO on down. In the previous personal example, my CEO made a point of tracking me down immediately after having lunch with my client, to comment on how much he enjoyed the time — and how much he appreciated the effort I took to calendar it for him. My client felt the exact same way. She was frankly honored that my CEO would take time out of his hectic schedule to meet in a long, one-on-one lunch with her.

On the second point, don't worry about promises that might be made or feedback that might be shared. If you prepare your management in advance, they won't say or promise anything that will compromise your hard work. And if you have built a strong client partnership, any potential client feedback will be positive on balance — which can only help you. During lunch with my CEO, my client shared some very positive comments about my team. In a business built on client relationships, this was good for my CEO to hear directly from my key client.

Frequently solicit client feedback

Client feedback is critically important to the process of building client partnerships. Solicit as much as you can as often as possible. You can't lead your clients without knowing how they feel, what they want, and how you can help them.

Practical tips:

- *During your routinely-scheduled breakfast, lunch or coffee meetings, you should consistently take the opportunity to solicit feedback.* Don't wait for your clients to offer an observation. Probe for feedback on your agency, the work, the people working on your team, and yourself.

- *If all you receive is positive feedback, don't just assume everything is okay.* Keep digging. Giving feedback is natural for some clients. But others are more hesitant. Especially with feedback that is critical. There must be something that can be improved. Politely push for it. Your clients will appreciate your genuine interest in continual improvement.

- *When clients do begin to offer feedback, be quiet and listen carefully.* Let them finish completely before responding. And don't take offense. If you interrupt your clients and/or become defensive, they will cease to provide future comments. This will severely inhibit your ability to build forward-moving partnerships.

- *Beyond listening, take action.* Show your clients you care about their feedback and you are willing and able to act on their concerns and suggestions. Develop a resolution plan — as mentioned in a previous chapter — to address the feedback. Share the plan with your clients, then share routine progress updates. Show your clients they can count on you. That you are a true partner. Remember, actions speaking louder than words. Clients don't tolerate client leaders who say all the right words, but deliver on nothing. They are quickly labeled "used-car salesmen." Don't let this happen to you. Deliver — or better yet, over-deliver — on your promises of improvement.

- *Make the process of sharing feedback easy on your clients.* Don't create work for them. At every agency in which I worked we solicited client feedback as part of our annual performance review process for individuals who engaged with clients. I strongly agree with the concept, but I disagreed with the typical recommended process. We were instructed to send to clients the same form we would employ to solicit internal cross-functional feedback. Personally, I felt it was terribly inappropriate to send clients a long input form and expect them to fill it out. We work for them, not the other way around. So, when I need to obtain client feedback on members of my team I offer to take my clients to a nice lunch. During lunch I simply ask them the questions and take notes (then fill out the form after lunch). By doing so I am able to attain better client feedback, because talking is much easier than filling out a form. And my clients very much appreciate the gesture. Moreover, it offers me yet another reason to connect live with my clients, which is always a good thing.

Personal example:

Actively soliciting critical feedback to improve a client partnership.

Our agency was suffering from a relatively poor and continually deteriorating relationship with our top client's internal design department, which controlled the relationship with us. We desperately needed to improve the situation — and do so with a proactive and robust plan.

As with any good plan, ours began with a situation analysis. We knew the relationship was not strong, but needed a more granular diagnostic understanding so we could address the situation with a detailed plan. To this end we conducted a survey of all the managers in the client's design department (over 150 people) via a direct mail execution. The tone of the survey was fun, yet sincere and unassuming — as depicted by the cover:

When flipped open, the piece read: "You love us not …" When flipped open one last time, it read: "Either way, we want to know." This was followed by an easy-to-complete survey. The client respondents simply needed to detach the survey from the body of the piece and mail it back. It was self-addressed and pre-stamped. We even included a nice pen for the clients to use and keep.

Partnership impact:

Because the survey was creative, fun and simple, we received an outstanding response rate (over 75%!). And the feedback was instrumental in helping us better understand the current situation and how it could be improved. In addition to developing a more vigorous feeling for the relationship in general, we were able to pinpoint particular issues that specific people were having (since we gave respondents the opportunity to identify themselves if they wanted, which the majority did). This allowed us to develop action plans tailored to individuals that could be executed in a personal manner by one of our team members. In a relationship-based business, it is much more effective to address issues on a one-to-one basis.

In addition, we were able to create a client segmentation model that grouped clients into distinct segments based on similar issues and opportunities. We then developed client communication plans based on these segmentation differences, rather than creating a mass communication plan in which all clients received the same messages (which is what most agencies do). For instance, if a particular segment of clients felt our creative was strong but our strategic thinking was sub-par, we would send this client segment success stories that showcased strong results from our strategic consultation. If another client segment felt the opposite, we would send it examples of beautiful creative work.

Here is an overview of the segmentation model:

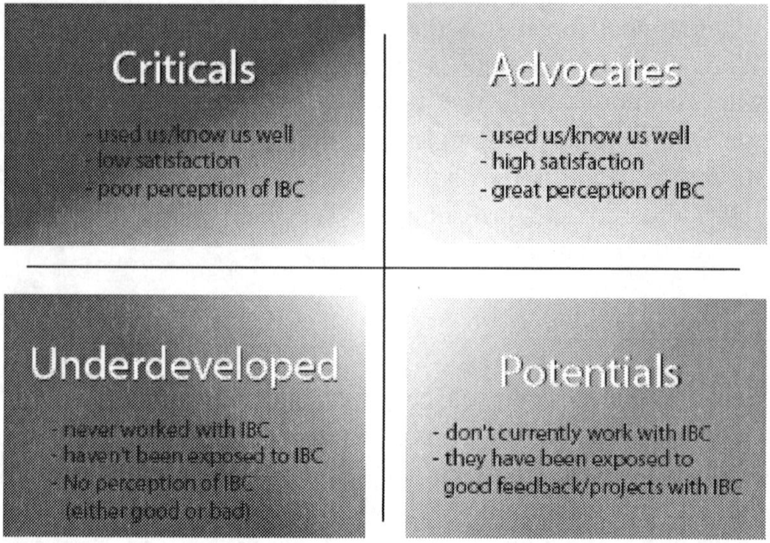

Criticals

- used us/know us well
- low satisfaction
- poor perception of IBC

Advocates

- used us/know us well
- high satisfaction
- great perception of IBC

Underdeveloped

- never worked with IBC
- haven't been exposed to IBC
- No perception of IBC (either good or bad)

Potentials

- don't currently work with IBC
- they have been exposed to good feedback/projects with IBC

Every year this client company would conduct a formal assessment of its roster agencies. Our performance review improved dramatically from the prior year after conducting this survey, and implementing the corresponding action plans. We were clearly successful in identifying key issues and addressing them effectively.

Turn clients into vocal advocates

As a client leader, and hence the face of your agency, you are responsible for representing your agency. This includes not just what you say about it, but what others say, too. You need to take control of as much messaging as possible.

Practical tips:

- *When you receive positive client feedback, take the time to truly show your appreciation.* I have found that clients don't take time to share positive feedback often, because they don't understand how much it is appreciated. Or, they assume you know how positively they feel about your work. So, when a client does share positive feedback, make sure they know full well how much it means to you. If they send the feedback via e-mail, don't just send a reply and say "thanks." In fact, don't reply via e-mail at all. Pick up the phone and let them hear your appreciation. If you make a big deal out of a small gesture, there will be no doubt about how much it means to you. The more gratitude you show, the more feedback you'll receive.

- *If clients share positive feedback with you, encourage them to share it with others, as well.* I have found that clients often don't think to share their feedback broadly. Either it simply doesn't occur to them or they don't think their feedback will matter much to other people. But, when asked to share it, clients are almost always happy to oblige. You need to make sure this is happening. Ensure your clients that their opinions do matter to other people and you truly appreciate when they share them.

<u>Personal example</u>:
Making the most of unsolicited, positive client feedback.

One particular day I received a nice e-mail from a key client about the great work our agency was doing on his behalf. Rather than sending an impersonal e-mail reply I immediately picked up the phone to thank him. I also encouraged him to share his complimentary feedback with his company's global design director, with whom we needed to build a stronger relationship. Because my client and I had such a strong relationship, he was more than happy to do so with the following note, which he sent the same day:

> *I do not believe you and I have formally met, but I am the brand manager for (Brand). Recently, as I'm sure you heard, (Brand) failed in its clinical trials. As part of the process of wrapping up our commercial work, we are capturing learnings on the business for what worked well and what didn't so we can continue to improve on future projects.*
>
> *As design lead in pharmaceuticals, I wanted to let you know one of the things we have done well is to hire [the right agency]. They were hired to develop a design theme and the trade dress. However, to get to the design theme, we had to get through the equity pyramid and brand character work first. This is where the agency exceeded expectations.*
>
> *To be honest, we were not sure what we could get; most of us thought of them as a design agency — talented, but*

not necessarily a strategic partner. Their familiarity with our company's processes and their strategic talents, though, allowed them to step into the role as a full strategic partner and help us develop equity pyramids and characters both our global president and VP/GM considered to be some of the best we've done.

My key point: [This agency] does excellent design work, but their talents are broader. They are a true strategic partner who has developed a wealth of pharmaceutical experience. As you create partnerships with core agencies, I strongly recommend them for the top of your list.

Please feel free to call me if you would like to know more.

Thanks.

Partnership impact:

As evidenced by this extremely positive note, it was certainly worth it for me to not only show my appreciation for my client's earlier thoughtful feedback, but to encourage him to share it more broadly. We had been trying to schedule an agency orientation meeting with the recipient of his note, but were unable to make it happen.

Following the delivery of this note, we were able to secure a meeting. At the beginning of the meeting, the recipient referenced our client's note — so it clearly had a positive impact on her. This was the launch of significant improvements in our partnership with this key client.

Immerse new clients immediately

The sooner you begin building relationships with new clients the better. Take the initiative to immerse new clients with a tremendous sense of urgency.

Practical tips:

- *As soon as you learn of a new manager addition to one of your client accounts, reach out to that person, introduce yourself, and offer to provide them with a thorough agency orientation to help immerse them in the business.* They will appreciate your enthusiasm to on-board them. Plus, this will help you control messaging about your agency. If they have not worked with your agency before, this offers you an opportunity to create an advantageous first impression. But, the longer you wait to orient new clients, the more they are likely to glean from other sources. Hopefully, they will hear good opinions, but you won't have control over the content.

- *Make the most of your first impression.* Let the clients see your enthusiastic passion for the business or brands they are joining. Make certain they see the great work you and your agency have been doing to nurture them — and your pride in it. Ensure that the new clients leave these initial meetings feeling quite comfortable that their business is in good hands — and knowing they can count on you.

- *Render the agency orientation about the clients, not just about your agency.* Share your capabilities, but do so in a manner that demonstrates how they have helped the clients' businesses in the past, and how you intend to continue contributing to their growth.

- *If you work with more than one client, as most client leaders do, you need to instill confidence in each client that they are important and they will receive the attention they deserve.* So, when introducing yourself to new clients for the first time, don't tell them all the other clients with whom you currently work. The new client will immediately begin to wonder how much of your time will be spent on them. To be clear, I am not instructing you to lie. If the new client asks, you must share with them a fully honest answer. I am simply suggesting that there is no need to bring it up unless the client does. You can and should tell them all the clients you have worked with *in the past*. This shows the new client that you have valuable experience — which will help build respect and confidence.

- *Supply new clients with an agency contact sheet, so they know who works on their businesses, what their role is, and how they can be contacted.* Don't ever make clients work to discover this information. And giving clients a stack of business cards from every member of the team is not enough; put all the contact information on one simple, easy-to-reference sheet.

Make clients feel welcome

When clients visit your office, whether for the first time or the hundredth, make them feel welcome the moment they step foot into your lobby. Enlist the help of everyone in your office to make sure this happens.

Practical tips:

- *Begin by creating a custom "Welcome (Client)" sign.* Have a member of your creative staff develop it so it looks professional. Some agencies have generic welcome signs. If your agency does, replace it with the custom sign during your clients' arrival periods. This is such a simple way to make your clients feel like you have been preparing for their arrivals, and that they are important to you and your agency. They are. This form of preparation will also show your clients that you are buttoned up and detail-oriented.

- *Ensure your lobby receptionist is expecting your clients' arrivals.* Provide a list of names and descriptions if necessary, so each member of the client team can be greeted not only with a friendly "hello," but also by name. And if your agency requires your visiting clients to wear temporary badges, have the receptionist create them in advance (with names spelled properly!). Another simple but powerful way to signal to your clients that you, and everyone in your agency, has prepared for their arrivals.

- *Provide your management with a "heads ups" that your clients are coming*. Even if your management will not be in the meeting, they can swing by at the beginning or end to shake hands and say "hi."

Participate in community service

As a client leader, you are the face of your agency. A great way to represent it is to participate in community service opportunities for which you possess true passion.

Practical tips:

- *Consider becoming involved in efforts in which you and your clients share a common interest.* This will provide an opportunity to help you build the personal aspect of your partnerships.

- *But, don't join a board or a group just because your clients are involved.* Be sincere and genuine. If you're not passionate about the effort and determined to create an impact, you will quickly be seen as a fraud who is merely trying to selfishly advance your personal interests. You need to focus on doing what is right.

Personal example:
Developing a community service program that benefited everyone involved.

One day I received a call from a former colleague of mine, who is now a professor at the University of Cincinnati. This professor was teaching a master's marketing course and wanted to see if I would be interested in talking to his MBA class about branding. We agreed to meet for breakfast to discuss the idea.

During our breakfast meeting I quickly decided there was much more we could do beyond simply arranging my presentation for this class. While in college I was awarded the opportunity to intern with P&G in brand management. This was an amazing experience for which I was and continue to be so thankful. Accordingly, I wanted to offer these students the best experience I could possibly provide. I suggested to my former colleague that we create an internship-type opportunity for his entire class, to impart real-world experience, not simply a lecture. He loved the idea.

To make the learning experience as robust as possible, we secured the involvement of my agency's largest client. This provided the students with a unique opportunity to learn about branding — from strategy development through creative execution — while working on a real project for a real brand.

We split the students into groups and created a competition, much like the TV show *The Apprentice.* Over the course of several weeks the students worked side-by-side with our strategic planners and graphic designers to learn about and develop branding campaigns.

Partnership impact:

This successful initiative was featured as a cover story in the *Cincinnati Business Courier*. Not only was this great PR for my agency, it was great PR for my client — providing yet another example of its community-oriented corporate citizenship. And the client did not have to do any work. My agency team took care of all the planning and execution.

Don't forget the little things

Little things can make a big difference. So keep the following miscellaneous tips top-of-mind.

- *Keep track of your clients as they move up the ladder and on to new companies.* You work too hard building partnerships with these people to let them slip away. Maximize your relationship building investments by staying in touch.

- *Learn from your peers.* Talk with them. Swap stories. Broaden your expertise by learning what's working and not working on other client accounts. Perspective is everything. Absorb as much of it as possible. The more diverse the better. Identify the best practices amongst your peers and leverage them with your clients, to grow their businesses.

- *Be accessible.* Your clients should know where you are and how to contact you. Update your voice-mail outgoing message so your clients know if you are in the office, in meetings, or traveling. Create automatic "out-of-office" notices in your e-mail program (personalize them and say "Hi" and "Thank you;" don't just engage the cold and impersonal default message). Provided your clients your mobile number. If you are going on vacation and won't be accessible, grant your clients as much advance notice as possible. And provide an alternative agency contact for their convenience.

- *Bring your PDAs to client meetings so follow-up meetings can be scheduled on the spot.* Don't say you need to go back to the office to check your calendar and get back to your clients with dates/times. That is inefficient and archaic.

- *Look the part.* Agency people should be in tune with contemporary societal trends. Dress professionally and with a sense of style. You don't have to do the stereotypical agency all-black thing. Stick with what works for you (unless that is khakis and flannel shirts!). Beyond your style of dress, show professionalism in other aspects of your appearance. Don't show up to client meetings with a cardboard-covered spiral notebook and cheap plastic pen. Buy a nice leather-bound notebook and stylish pen. Look like a consultant, not a college student. Lastly, carry a nice bag, portfolio, or brief case. Don't tuck artwork or presentation boards under your arm and head off to client meetings (I have seen it done!).

- *Be early to meetings.* This seems so obvious, but it is abused too often by agency people. And it drives clients crazy. If it takes 30 minutes to drive to your client's office, don't allow for *only* 30 minutes. Arriving at the parking lot on time is not sufficient. You need to check in with the lobby receptionist, walk to the conference room, and set up ahead of the scheduled time; and be ready to begin the second the client walks in the room.

- *If your client's company requires visitors to wear badges — and there is an opportunity to secure a permanent badge to avoid needing your client to act as an escort for you — make sure everyone on the agency team has a permanent one.* Don't make your client come down to the reception area to escort you and your team back up to his or her office, simply because one member of your agency team doesn't have a permanent badge. Be considerate.

- *Guard your clients' confidential business information like it is your own.* Shred documents. Don't share information with anyone who doesn't need to see it. Don't talk about it in public places. If your agency wants to showcase its successful work with one client by sharing it with other clients, mask it appropriately (as done throughout this book). I recently heard a horror story about a client president overhearing an agency person discussing their confidential work on an airplane. The client chastised him publicly on the spot. Don't be that person!

- *Develop an "elevator speech."* Be able to articulate the unique benefits of your agency in 30 seconds or less. And be ready to share it any time you are asked by current or prospective clients, "What do you *do*?"

- *Send personalized holiday cards.* Don't be idle and simply rely on the standard, generic cards (or e-mails) your agency likely sends to clients. Send your own. Be personal with your client partners. Every year my wife and I hand-make holiday cards featuring our kids. I send these cards not only to family and friends, but to my clients. And I include a personal note thanking them for their partnerships. Every year clients tell me how much they appreciate this personal touch.

- *Maintain a healthy mind and body.* Okay, this last tip may seem a bit "out there." But, it is one that I have learned to appreciate increasingly, the older I become. Being a client leader is a very demanding job. One that requires lots of energy and a consistently positive outlook.

You need to be in good physical and mental shape. To accomplish this, my foremost tip is to exercise routinely. Add to that a healthy and balanced diet. Strike a manageable work/life balance to avoid burn-out. Spend time with family and friends. Pursue hobbies and other purposeful diversions. Find ways to manage stress and anxiety that work for you. Consider things like yoga, breathing exercises, aromatherapy, and music therapy. This may seem a bit wacky, but don't knock it 'till you try it! Everyone in this business experiences stress. The more you can control it, the more effective and happy you will be, both personally and professionally.

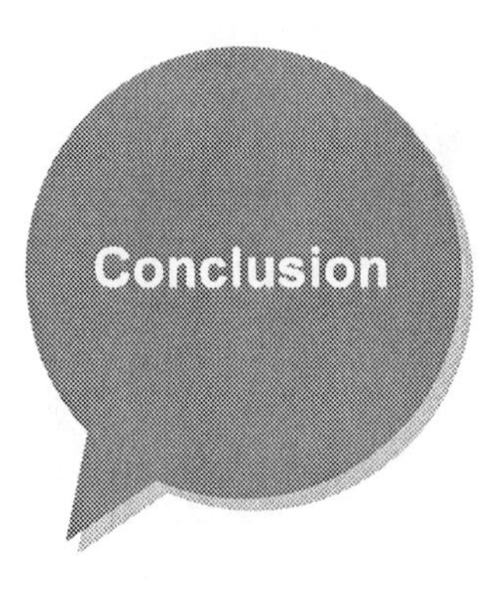

Thank you for taking the time to read and consider my thoughts and practical tips for how you can become a passionate and proactive partner to your clients. I hope you found this perspective helpful and will refer back to it often.

As I have noted throughout *Tell Your Clients Where to Go!*, I encourage you to seek out and learn continually from as much diverse perspective as possible. There is no perfect blueprint for becoming an outstanding partner. This book is just one piece of perspective from which you will hopefully profit.

Remember, you are the face of your agency. Maintain this mindset at all times, attack your role in a passionate and proactive manner, continually develop other quintessential qualities and skills, and apply some of the practical tips provided in this book. If you do so, I guarantee you will never be seen as an "order taker!" To the contrary, you will be well on your way to becoming an indispensable partner to your clients.

Good luck!

One of the tips in this book about which I am particularly passionate is maintaining good manners. This includes saying "thank you." So, I would be remiss if I didn't take a moment to acknowledge some people who have been particularly helpful and special to me throughout my personal life and professional career.

Meaningful mentors

I was blessed with amazing guidance as I began my career on both the client and agency sides of the marketing and communications business. While in college I experienced the incredible opportunity to intern in brand management at Procter & Gamble. I was only 19 years old and didn't possess a single relative clue! So I was incredibly fortunate to benefit from the mentorship of **Mark Macchiarulo**, now president of Amplitude Marketing Group. Beyond his incredible intelligence and strategic thinking, he is a master at tactfully cutting through bureaucratic b.s. and making things happen. If he hadn't taken me under his wing, I shutter to think where I would be today.

I switched to the agency side of the industry several years later, and was very fortunate to learn from **Susan Jones**. Her ability to form long-term, win-win client partnerships is simply unparalleled. She immediately opened my eyes to how to become an outstanding agency partner, and never stopped teaching me. Her lessons continue to impact my behavior to this day, every day.

Impressive client partners

Great client relationships can't be formed without great clients. I have been blessed with the opportunity to work with some of the most talented clients in the business. Folks like **Doug Stuckey**, a long-time veteran of Procter & Gamble. He taught me so much about both sides of the business. He consistently rewards good work with more work. And he always makes work fun.

Norm Ellard, another veteran of Procter & Gamble, is so comfortable in yielding to the agency's expertise. As a result, he always inspires us to do our best work. And he is a very loyal client.

Joey Bergstein, SVP at Diageo, is always very challenging to please. But, when he is pleased, he is incredibly complimentary. Working with him is extremely fulfilling.

Steve Tebeau and **Michelle St. John**, co-owners of Inner-Circle — a very successful live marketing agency — are always demanding, but at the same time, unbelievably appreciative of good work. They quickly turned from clients, into two of my best friends to this day.

Greg Zimmer, chief brand designer at 3M, is a very open, honest, and transparent client. And he always goes out of his way to promote and champion great work.

April Anslinger is one of the most passionate clients I have ever met and as a result, one of my all-time favorites. She has very high expectations, as she should. And if they are not met, she makes it very clear. But, she is also very compassionate and more than willing to roll up her sleeves to help the agency address her issues. She is the epitome of a perfect client partner.

Robert Cleveland and **Ena Singh** are two of the most sincere and supportive clients with whom I have had the pleasure to work. Their partnership approach always generates great work, and they always make sure other folks hear about the effective results.

Finally, I want to thank **James Pratt**. A very skilled leader and communicator who always benefits the agency with strategic, inspirational and actionable feedback that makes the work significantly better. In true form, he also provided a tremendous amount of helpful feedback on the manuscript for this book.

Passionate creative partners

If you work in an agency or professional services firm that develops creative work for clients, it is imperative that you have outstanding creatives who love their chosen profession. And it is imperative that you form great partnerships with them. I have worked with so many talented creative folks in my career. But, three stand out for the rewarding partnership they afforded me.

Gary Whitlock and I were extremely successful partners at Interbrand, where he was the chief creative officer. I have never witnessed a better presenter than Gary. Clients literally hang on his every word. He is truly gifted at educating clients in both brand strategy and design, not selling to them. By the time he is through presenting, clients feel like they would be foolish not to adhere to his recommendations.

John Walsh is the most analytical and detail-oriented creative it has been my pleasure to know. He is also extremely caring, and this combination of skills and personal qualities garners an unmatched level of trust and respect.

Finally, when it comes to forming client relationships, **Tim Fening's** prowess is practically unmatched. In fact, he is a better account person than the majority of account folks I have come across in this business. He is also a highly-skilled and experienced creative, and makes the creative development process painless and fun.

Talented team members

Leading account teams has always been the most fulfilling part of my job. I love coaching and training — and seeing folks grow as a result. And I love the fact that I have hired and trained countless talented people who have helped me learn and grow, in return. I would like to thank those who have had a particularly strong impact on me, who have been very loyal, and who have been forgiving and understanding friends. They include: **Amanda Skerski**, for her open-mindedness to learn and her flowing appreciation when she does; **Chris Ertel**, for his hunger for feedback and his hell-bent desire to grow from it; **Rob Jones**, for his confidence in challenging me and making me a better leader; **Kelly Tholke** and **Robyn Van Rens**, for their unwavering positive attitudes and pleasant smiles; **Daphne Wedig** for her creative "can do" spirit; and **Terry Phillips** and **Brian Higdon**, for their brilliant minds and consultative approaches that improve client perceptions.

Enthusiastic endorsers

Words cannot accurately articulate my appreciation for the numerous industry leaders who took precious time out of their hectic schedules to read my manuscript and offer helpful advice and supportive praise. *I will never forget your generosity.* **John E. Pepper**, **James Pratt, Matthew Fenton** and **Todd Henry** deserve special recognition for the particularly strong inspiration, guidance and support they provided to help make this project a success.

And last but certainly not least ... God. He is the ultimate leader and partner! Without God's grace I wouldn't have the experiences, successes, failures, and perspective that have enabled me to write this book and hopefully help others. For this reason I am donating 100% of my income from this book to charities dedicated to God's great work.

Todd Sebastian is vice president, client leadership at dunnhumby, the world's leading shopper and consumer insights consulting firm. Prior to joining dunnhumby he spent several successful years at Interbrand, an Omnicom brand strategy and design agency. Todd joined as vice president, group account director and was promoted to chief account officer of the Cincinnati office before moving up to executive director of North America. He started his career in brand management at Procter & Gamble, and prior to Interbrand, held senior-level positions in the advertising industry. Todd has been recognized in the *Who's Who in Greater Cincinnati Advertising, PR & Design* and featured numerous times in the *Greater Cincinnati Business Courier*, in addition to other business and trade publications. He lives in Cincinnati with his wife, Kathy, and two children, Sydney and Dean.